MISTAKES

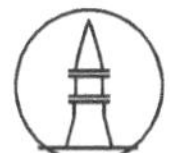

First published by The Frankfort Press in 2026
www.frankfortpress.com

Title: Mistakes. Carried & Abandoned
Author: Unknown
Orchestrated by: Andrew Hollister

These pages come from imagination and memory. Some names are real, some are not. What appears here is offered with care.

ISBN: 979-8-218-93660-0

This book was printed in the United States.

MISTAKES
CARRIED & ABANDONED

Orchestrated by
A.M.HOLLISTER

THE FRANKFORT PRESS
EST. 1798

"Uncertainty is an uncomfortable position.
But certainty is an absurd one."

—Voltaire

22 March 2025

I found these notebooks in a crate beside the bench. Some were written like instructions. Others like arguments with no one in the room.

The paper varies. Early pages are thin and brittle, corners softened by handling. Later ones grow heavier, the margins tighter. Ink darkens, then fades. A few pages are water-stained. One section is stuck together badly enough that I couldn't separate it without tearing the paper. I left it that way.

There are repetitions. Whole ideas returned to, crossed out, written again. Dates revised. Handwriting steadies, then slips.

I can't say when he meant these notes to be read, or if he ever did. I only know they were kept, moved, and added to over years. I've left them largely as I found them. What's missing stays missing.

—A

PART 1

The Work Begins

Why bother?

or, Where the sawdust and the stubbornness begin.

They say a tidy workshop is the mark of a restless mind. I say it usually means a man is avoiding something else.

I have swept a bench clean more times than I can count without having any intention of starting new work. Push broom from left to right. Scoop the pile. Miss a corner on purpose so there is still something to do. A clean bench looks like readiness. Most days it is just delay.

The shop smells the same whether anything gets built or not. Wood dust. Oil. Old glue. Sometimes coffee that went cold because I forgot it was there. You can stand in that smell a long time without deciding anything.

This work is slow. Not patient. Slow. It tightens your shoulders and leaves your hands feeling older than they are. Some days the boards fight you. Some days they sit there like they are waiting to see what kind of mood you brought in with you. Every now and then the grain catches the light and looks like it might be trying to tell you something. It never is.

I am not a master. I have ruined more pieces than I have saved. I have walked out of shops mid-afternoon because I could not stand the sight of what I had done to a good board. I have left clamps on overnight that did not need to be there, just so the work would still look unfinished in the morning.

What I know is how to stay in a room longer than I want to. How to stand there with a board that does not care what you hoped for, and decide to make the next cut anyway

That is why we start with a box.

No curves. No tricks. No brass feet. Nothing that hides. Four sides, a bottom, a lid if you are feeling ambitious. A piece of walnut that does not know you. A bench that will not help you. Enough stubbornness to stay put until something holds.

The box does not ask who you are. It only asks if you will stay long enough to finish something.

★ ★ ★

The reason we do this, instead of something easier.

or, The bar fight that started everything.

Cole's Tavern was not the kind of place you planned to be. You ended up there because it was open and because the stools were bolted to the floor. The beer was cold enough. The lights stayed low even during the day. The bartender Sarge, or maybe it was Richie, had a way of wiping the same spot on the counter while listening to things he had already heard.

I was nineteen. Close enough to twenty-one to get served if I didn't talk too much. Old enough to know better. Young enough to think that mattered.

There was nothing special about the night. No long

story. Someone bumped into me. Words followed. Then hands. I remember the sound my head made when it hit the floor. I remember the taste of blood and pennies. I remember thinking, briefly, that this was not how anything was supposed to start.

My father did not ask what happened. He set a canvas bag of tools on the kitchen table and waited until I sat down. My lip was split. One eye was already swelling.

"Make yourself useful," he said.

That was it.

The next morning I went into the shop. I stood there for a while without turning anything on. The house behind me was loud in a way I did not want to name. The shop was quieter. The bench did not care what I looked like.

I picked up a board and cut it too short. I cut another one wrong. I glued my fingers together and pulled them apart without swearing. By late afternoon there was something on the bench that resembled a box if you did not look too closely.

It was ash. Four sides and a bottom. The corners did not meet the way they were supposed to. One side bowed out just enough to catch your eye. There was a glue blotch I could not scrape away without making it worse. I sanded until the edges went soft.

I did not think about what it meant. I did not think about craft, or honesty or any of the other words people use when they are trying to explain themselves. I just kept going back into the shop. I went back the next day. And the day after that. Some days I worked. Some days I just stood there and moved things around until the light changed. I swept the floor even when it did not need it. I left the radio off. The shop stayed quiet. The house did not.

I did not tell anyone I was building boxes. I did not give the first one away. I slid it under the bench and left it there. When I walked past Cole's Tavern again, about a week later, I crossed the street without thinking about it.

The shop was easier.

On boredom, perfection, and the box.

or, Why the quiet part is the hardest.

The first box sat under the bench longer than it needed to. I told myself I was letting the glue cure. Then that the finish needed time. Then nothing at all. It stayed there because I did not know what else to do with it.

I would pull it out some mornings and turn it in my hands. The corners were not square. One side had a faint twist that showed up when the light hit it just right. The bottom rattled if you shook it. I could fix some of it. I knew that. I also knew that fixing one thing would make another worse. So I set it back under the bench and pretended that was a decision.

Boredom shows up early in this work. Not the kind you talk about. The other kind. The kind that settles in your shoulders and makes you check the clock without knowing why. You sand because sanding fills time. You sand past the pencil line and then wonder why you bothered marking it in the first place.

I learned to make excuses that sounded responsible. Let the wood acclimate. Check the humidity. Clean the tools. Rearrange the shelves. I sharpened a chisel that did not need it. I sharpened it again because it felt better than making a cut I might regret.

Perfection never entered my mind as a goal. I did not know the word well enough yet. What I knew was hesitation. The feeling that if I touched the box again I would have to admit where I had gone wrong.

It was easier to stand there and look busy.

The shop stayed quiet. The radio stayed off. I could hear the scrape of sandpaper and the small sound the box made when I set it down too hard. Outside, people came and went. I noticed the light change. I noticed my hands were sore in a way they had not been before.

Eventually I wiped the box down and called it finished. Not because it was right. Because I was tired of moving around it. I slid it back under the bench and swept the floor. The dust went where it always does. The shop looked the same as it had that morning.

I did not feel proud or disappointed.

Just done.

The next day I started another box.

★ ★ ★

Perfecting miters.

or, The jewelry box Patsy burned.

A miter joint looks honest until you ask it to close. Two clean cuts. One simple angle. Nothing hiding. Then you bring the pieces together and see daylight where there shouldn't be any. Sometimes it sings. Sometimes it shows your hand.

I've watched grown men lose whole afternoons chasing perfect forty-fives. Convinced the saw was faithful, never noticing the fence had crept.

Wood moves. Saws pretend they don't notice. Mostly we rush and hope glue will negotiate.

The first miter I ever cut looked fine until it didn't. Both ends proud. The corner open just enough to laugh at me. I said the wood was wrong. My father didn't argue. He put the board back in my hands and waited. That pause did more work than any lecture ever could.

Lessons From the Line

1. Do not trust factory angles. The 90 on your saw is decoration until you prove it. Tune the sled. Shim if needed. Test cuts are cheap. Regret isn't.
2. Cut long first. Sneak up on final length. One hair too short and your corner will look like a missing tooth.
3. Same side, same setup. Cut both matching pieces without moving the stop. Move the stop and the symmetry dies.
4. Dry fit under pressure. Tape it. Clamp it. Then swear at it. Only then do you learn what the glue up will become.
5. Fix it now or stare at it forever. If there's a gap, stop. Slice a sliver. Shim with the same board. Do it right and you can fool the eye. Do it wrong and you will see that corner every time you pass the damn thing.
6. Burn the mock up if its off. A clean slate beats a living reminder.

Patsy lived down in the valley, Holland Patent. His barn smelled like oil and pine. He built planes the way other men build excuses, slowly and without apology. I learned more standing near him than I ever did asking questions.

He once took a whole jewelry box, fine wood, polished to a dull shine, and pitched it into the stove. A single corner was off. He watched it burn and said miters are like old friendships. One bad angle and it all falls apart. Folks said he wasn't well. He was clear enough for me.

You either fix it clean or you live with it.

Twenty years later, I'd done both.

Every shop I left. Every town I quit.

Another corner I didn't want to stare at.

★ ★ ★

The brass abyss with hinge mortising.

or, How the last inch takes everything.

Here's the thing about hinges. They come last, and they do not care how well you behaved before. You can spend days getting the box right. Miters closed. Panels flat. Shellac laid down clean. Then you take a sharp tool to finished work and find out what you really know.

Hinges demand precision the way gravity does. Quietly. Without appeal. You get one depth. One alignment. One chance to keep the lid from leaning like it lost interest halfway through life.

The old solid brass ones are the worst, which is to say the best. Heavy. Square. Unforgiving. They do not tolerate wobble or guesswork. They do not compress. They do not forgive enthusiasm. If you freehand, they will let you know.

There are a few tools worth keeping close. Sharp chisels, the kind that cut true without ceremony. A marking knife that leaves a line you can feel. A router plane or a guide block if your hands are not steady yet. Brass screws, soft enough to punish carelessness. We will come back to those.

Every time I open the hinge drawer, I see my collection of broken screws. Heads snapped. Threads torn. Brass too soft to forgive rushing.

The Process: Measure Twice, Then Panic

1. Dry fit the hinge. Do not guess thickness. Use the actual hinge. Mark around it with a knife, not a pencil. This is not a suggestion.
2. Scribe deep. Deep enough to register your chisel. Not so deep you cut a divorce line through your back panel.
3. Chisel the perimeter first. Work inward. Take your time. If your hand shakes, stop. Drink some water. Sit down. Come back.
4. Clear the waste slowly. Shallow passes. Layer by layer. Think of it like uncovering a fossil. One that does not like you.
5. Test fit often. Do not force it. Brass compresses nothing. It simply wins.
6. Pilot every hole. These screws are made of antique soap. If you do not pilot, lubricate, and treat them with respect, one will snap off flush. Then you will stare at it. Then you will curse. Then you will consider taking up another hobby.

Just remember, what you screw up at the end undoes all you did at the start.

The grace of the patch.

or, Making peace with imperfection before it grows teeth.

The piece was done. Then it cracked. Not a dramatic split. Nothing loud. Just a thin line running with the grain, easy to miss unless the light hit it wrong. I set the box down and walked past it twice before I stopped pretending I hadn't seen it.

I tried to tell myself it would close. That a little finish would calm it down. Wood likes to move. Everyone knows that. Sometimes it settles. Sometimes it doesn't. This one didn't.

I set the box back on the bench and stared at the crack long enough to learn nothing new about it. It wasn't wide enough to wedge glue into without making a mess. Not clean enough to ignore. It sat there, quiet and patient, waiting for me to decide how honest I felt like being.

The first patch came from the wrong scrap. Wrong color. Wrong grain. I tried it anyway. It sat proud on one side and disappeared on the other. I pried it out before the glue set and tossed it.

The second patch caught the light differently. I pressed it in dry and ran my thumb across the seam. You could feel it if you were looking for it.

Nick wandered by while I was fitting the patch, checking the grain match before committing to glue. He watched without saying anything until I stopped.

"You could've hidden it," he said.

I nodded. He wasn't wrong. A dutchman cut

tighter. A little filler. Careful sanding. No one would have known unless they went looking.

He looked at it a little longer, and then moved on.

I glued it in and left it alone longer than I needed. When I came back, I planed it flush in thin passes, stopping more often than usual.

The patch never disappeared.

I didn't try to make it invisible.

The color was close enough. The fit was clean. The line stayed visible if you knew where to look.

I finished the box and set it on the shelf with the others. From across the room it looked fine. Up close, another story.

I didn't know yet what that meant. I only knew I'd see it every time I picked it up. And that I'd chosen not to hide it.

★ ★ ★

Burn marks and blunt blades.

or, When it all goes to hell and you probably deserve it.

The burn showed up before I smelled it. A dark line along the edge where the blade had lingered too long. Not a gouge. Not a slip. Just heat doing what heat does when you don't stop it. I lifted the board and turned it, hoping the mark would change its mind. It didn't.

I told myself I could sand it out. That's what everyone says first. I hit it with eighty grit and watched the surface lighten while the line stayed put. I went to sixty and made a mess. By the time I stepped back, the board was thinner than it should have been and the burn was still there. Faint. Still there.

The blade had been dull. I knew that. I'd known it before the cut and kept going anyway. Sharpening takes time. Stopping feels like losing momentum. I convinced myself one more pass wouldn't matter.

I changed blades and tried again on a fresh board. The cut went through clean and quiet. No smoke. No scorch. I set the burned one aside, meaning to come back to it later. It joined a growing stack leaning against the wall. Boards that were almost right. Boards that would be useful someday. Boards that carried the cost of a decision I didn't want to interrupt.

The stack grew faster than I admitted.

Burn marks teach you about heat.

Blunt blades teach you about patience.

Mostly they teach you how long you're willing to pretend the problem is something else. I sharpened when the blade refused to cut. Not when it started to complain.

Patsy caught me forcing a plane across a panel one afternoon. The iron skated and left chatter where there shouldn't have been any.

"Sharp fixes most things," he said, without looking up.

I nodded and kept going until the plane stopped behaving altogether. Then I set it down harder than I needed to. The sound echoed longer than the mistake deserved. I sharpened that night until my hands were sore. Took too much off the iron and had to reset the whole thing. When I finally put it back to wood, the cut was clean enough to make me angry. All that trouble for something I could have done hours earlier.

The burned board stayed in the corner. I didn't throw it out. I didn't fix it either. It reminded me what happens when you work past the point where attention slips and pride takes over. I learned to read the sound of a blade before it failed. The thin whine as it moved through a cut. I didn't always listen. But I noticed.

Sharp fixes most things.
Doesn't fix where you put your hands.

I lost the tip of my left pinky in '87. Table saw. White oak. I was ripping stock and my hand drifted a quarter inch closer than it should have. The blade didn't pause. Didn't negotiate. Just took what was in its path and kept spinning.

When I messed up, I fixed the wood instead of trying to disguise the damage. Cut a patch from the same board. Matched the grain. Fit it square. Glued it tight. Planed it flush. Then kept going.

That finger never grew back.

Glue-up without regret.

or, How to wrestle time, gravity, and squeeze-out into submission.

You've cut your miters. You've shellac'd the inner panels to a mirror shine. You've rehearsed your dry fit like a nervous actor in a one-man show. And now? Now you get one shot. One wet, slippery, no-take backs moment to bring the whole damn thing together.

You only truly know yourself when the glue starts setting and nothing fits. Learned that the hard way, more than once.

Glue-up is where the confident turn quiet and the wise get twitchy. You're fighting open time, alignment, clamping pressure, and the eternal mystery of why the hell won't that last corner close?

This is why I switched to hide glue years ago. Gives you twenty minutes instead of five, and when you inevitably mess it up, a little heat and steam brings it back to life. Tomorrow's another chance. Read that in an old book from 1935, called "Doing The Gluing" by Keystone, taught me that. The best fifty cents I ever spent at an estate sale.

Prepping for the Battle

1. Tape the miters. Painter's tape, edge to edge, like hinges made of hope. Dry fit. Fold it up like origami. This is your rehearsal dinner. Don't drink at it.

2. Prevent squeeze out in the finish zones. Tape off those inner shellac'd panels like you're masking for war. One drop of Titebond on your polish and you'll spend the rest of the day mumbling.
3. Choose the right glue. Yellow glue is fine. Hide glue if you're a romantic masochist, like me. Just remember: glue waits for no one. Know your working time.
4. Have all clamps at the ready. Not nearby. Not "I'll grab them when I need them." Ready. Like firemen at a five-alarm blaze.

The moment of truth

1. Apply the glue. Thin and fast. Too much and you'll be chasing joints like a cat trying to cover shit on a marble floor. Too little and the box will die of loneliness.
2. Fold and clamp. Start at opposite corners, move quickly, apply pressure like you mean it. If it starts to twist, you didn't dry fit enough. Don't cry. Yet.
3. Check for square. Measure diagonals. Curse under your breath. Tap gently. This is where prayers and shims go to work.
4. Clean the squeeze out, but not too early. Wait for it to gel. Scrape with a chisel. Wipe it too soon and you're just spreading despair.

If it goes wrong, and it will, sure as rain, you'll find yourself staring at a corner that won't budge. One panel standing proud like a secret you didn't mean to keep. You'll peer into that gap and wonder if maybe you're fooling yourself.

You're not.

You cut a sliver. A small mercy from the same board. You slip it in. Then you plane it smooth, sanding the fault away like a man trying to make peace with himself.

Every glue-up teaches the same lesson. Hold things firmly. Hold them long enough. And let the rest settle where it may.

The bottom nobody talks about.

or, The poem no one was meant to find.

You didn't think about the bottom. You were busy fussing over book matching grain and cutting dovetails. Picking the perfect piece for the lid. Imagining how the finish would catch the light and make the whole thing feel intentional. You gave the bottom a passing thought and told yourself you'd deal with it later.

Later shows up fast.

You flip the box over and there it is. A slapped-on offcut. A loose dado, so the panel shifts when you lift it. The underside no one sees, except you. Except the day someone else does.

It happens. We all get seduced by the parts people admire. The show surfaces. The edges that catch a hand or an eye. The bottom feels like housekeeping. Necessary. Uninteresting. Easy to rush.

But the thing about the bottom, it remembers.

One day someone will pick up the box to dust under it. Or move it from one shelf to another. Or inherit it and turn it over out of curiosity. They'll run a finger along the grain and feel the hesitation you left there. The shortcut. The moment you decided close enough was good enough because no one was watching.

They won't know your reasons. They won't know the hour or the mood or what you were trying to finish before dark. They'll just know that something was done in a hurry.

I've found notes that way. Hidden where no one thought to look. Scraps of handwriting on the backs of pages. Margins filled because the front was already spoken for.

The underside records it.

Sanding as a spiritual practice.

or, Where he learned to stop before the work told him to.

Sanding is where the drama ends.

The cuts are done. The joints are set. Nothing loud remains. What's left is friction and time, and whether you can stand to be alone with both.

I used to rush it. Everyone does. Sanding feels like punishment for earlier mistakes. You tell yourself you're just smoothing, but really you're trying to erase evidence. The scratch you missed. The glue line you swore wouldn't show. The corner you softened too much because you lost patience.

The paper does not care.

It clogs. It dulls. It tears when you push too hard. If you lean into it, it bites back. If you stay light, it asks you to stay longer. That's the bargain. There is no shortcut that doesn't announce itself later under finish.

You learn the grits the way you learn a walk. Coarse enough to matter. Fine enough to forgive. Skip one and the surface remembers. Run your finger across it, your hands will see it before your eyes.

I sand by hand more than I should. Not because it's efficient. Because it tells me when to stop. Machines are eager. They'll keep going long after the work is done. Hands get tired. They start to complain. That's useful information.

There's a point when the surface stops fighting you. The grain settles. The edges stop grabbing light. You wipe the dust away and nothing jumps out. No heroics. No shine. Just calm.

That's when most people quit.

They shouldn't.

The last passes matter. The ones that don't seem to change anything. That's where you decide whether you're finishing or just moving on. I've ruined good work by being in a hurry to be done with it.

So you keep going.

Even when it feels like nothing is happening.

Even when the work refuses to reward you.

When the dust finally settles and there's nothing left to chase, you're not proud. You're quiet. And that's usually the sign it's ready.

Shellac & French Polish.

or, Twenty coats and a woman in Cooperstown.

Shellac isn't just some finish you slap on and forget. No sir. It's a reckoning. A slow, stubborn reckoning. Anybody can drown a board in poly with a foam brush and walk off feeling like they beat the world. But shellac? Shellac wants a conversation. A long one. It'll make you wait, make you work, rub and build and circle back and apologize like the night's never going to end.

She's moody. Wild. She remembers everything you do to her. And when she finally sings, man, there is nothing else like it.

A glow that doesn't just shine, but remembers.

I learned shellac the hard way. Too thick and you get ridges. Too thin and you might as well use spit. Humidity over sixty percent? Pour yourself three fingers of bourbon and come back tomorrow.

Some days the flakes dissolve. Some days they sulk. Some days the jar just sits there teaching you patience whether you asked for it or not.

But when the conditions line up, when the air behaves, when your hand remembers what to do without you telling it, the finish goes down like butter and the grain jumps out like it's showing off. That's the moment you remember why you bother with this fussy old-world bullshit instead of just buying polyurethane and calling it a day.

French polishing isn't about hiding the wood.

It's about layering something so thin it barely exists, yet somehow makes the surface more real. Like dusting off an old truth. Like uncovering something that was already there and pretending you had anything to do with it.

Shellac doesn't reward speed.

It rewards staying.

And it only gives itself to people who are willing to come back tomorrow.

The Setup: Get It Right or Regret It

1. Cut. One pound shellac. Start there. Go thinner if the wood or your pride can't take it.
2. Solvent. Pure alcohol. Or Everclear. None of the denatured garbage from the gas station.
3. Rubber. Clean linen wrapped around wool. Not a paper towel, or a damn sock. This isn't summer camp.
4. Oil. A touch of olive or walnut. Enough to let the pad glide. Too much and you lose control.

Shellac works on its own schedule. Rush it and you'll get streaks. Hesitate too long and it'll tack up and punish you. The old guys mixed their cuts by feel. One pound. Two pound. Whatever looked right in the jar that morning. Not science. Practice.

You learn to work in thin coats because thick ones never dry clean. You learn to stop before it looks finished. You learn to wait.

The Process: Like Prayer With Elbow Grease

1. Load the pad. But not too much. Damp, not dripping. It's not a BBQ mop.
2. Spirits pass. Straight alcohol to prep the grain and your attitude. Removes smudges and hubris.
3. Circular motion or figure eights. Doesn't matter, as long as you stay consistent and don't think about lunch.
4. Let it rest. Shellac isn't speed dating. Let it cure. Come back later with grace.
5. Cut back with 0000 steel wool. Gently. Like apologizing to someone you wronged in '87. Repeat until you question reality. Somewhere between eight and twenty sessions, you will either find enlightenment. Or quit.

I once spent three weeks polishing a jewelry box meant for a woman in Cooperstown. Her name was Leta, and she laughed like she didn't expect anyone to hear it. Cherry. Brass hinges I'd been saving for something important. By coat twelve, I knew I wasn't going to give it to her. By coat twenty, I was packing the truck. The box is still in a drawer somewhere. Perfect finish.

French polishing doesn't hide mistakes. It layers forgiveness so thin it almost disappears. The surface remembers every pass, every pause, every day you showed up and every day you didn't.

That's why I still use it. Not because it's beautiful. Because it keeps a record.

★ ★ ★

Knowing when you're done, even if you're not.

or, The question the wood keeps asking.

There gets to a certain point when the work stops asking more questions.

That doesn't mean it's finished.

It means it's tired of you.

You can feel it when every adjustment makes something else worse. When sanding no longer improves the surface, only changes it. When the finish looks different in every light and none of them tell you what to do next. That's the moment people mistake for failure.

It isn't.

It's the work telling you it has given what it can. The rest belongs to time, use, and whoever lives with it next.

I didn't know that early on. I thought being done meant arriving somewhere clean. Final. Decisive. I kept touching things long after they were ready, chasing a version that only existed in my head. I dulled edges that were meant to stay sharp. I softened corners that needed tension. I turned honest work into something polite.

The hardest part isn't stopping because it looks bad. It's stopping when it looks good enough to tempt you into one more pass.

That last pass is where most pieces lose themselves.

I've learned to leave small things unresolved. A faint tool mark under the finish. A corner that asks for attention without demanding it. Not as a statement. As a boundary. Proof that I knew when to walk away.

Being done doesn't feel like satisfaction. It feels like restraint. Like putting something down even though you could keep going. Like admitting that whatever comes next won't make it truer.

Some things aren't finished. They're released.

Released doesn't mean resolved.

It means you stop touching it before it asks for more than you can give.

It means you leave with questions still hanging, edges still sharp enough to catch.

It means accepting that whatever comes next won't make it truer.

And that has to be enough.

★ ★ ★

The monsoon hammers the tin roof of this shop in Chiang Mai, while I'm learning to sharpen on water stones. The old man running this place doesn't speak English, I don't speak Thai, but we both understand what happens when steel meets stone at the wrong angle. He's teaching me patience through repetition. Same stroke, same pressure, hour after hour.

Outside, a radio is playing Born to Run. Strange what travels. I came here running from something back home, ended up sitting still for the first time in five years. Learning that you can't sharpen anything, neither blade nor man, while you're moving.

When I nail the angle just right, the old man gives me a nod and lights up another Krong Thip. The smoke mingles with the wet earth smell, and I think, three months from now, I'll take what he's taught me and bring back a No. 4 Stanley plane that'll last longer than either of us.

PART II

Mistakes, Lessons, and the Doing Years

The pages that follow are messier than the first set. More cross-outs. More restarts. A few entries written on the backs of receipts and torn envelopes, the ink pressed hard enough to leave an impression on the sheet beneath.

Some pieces repeat with small changes, as if he kept returning to the same trouble to see if it would tell him something different. I've left that repetition intact.

—A

The first tool I ever stole.

or, Loud dumb and the sound it makes.

It wasn't a valuable tool. That's how I justified it later. A small block plane with a nicked iron and a handle polished smooth by someone else's hand. The kind of thing you notice because it's missing, not because it's special.

I was working for Mr. Vicker at the time. Odd jobs. Shop cleanup. Carrying things that weighed more than they should have. He didn't watch closely. He didn't need to. The place ran on habit and assumption. Tools went back where they belonged because that's what people did. Until they didn't.

I slipped the plane into the inside pocket of my coat while he was on the phone. Shearling. I'd had it a year and it still felt stolen itself. No rush. No cover. Just a quiet decision made faster than it deserved. I remember thinking I'd bring it back once I had a chance to tune it properly. Make it better than I found it. As if that mattered.

I was young. I was dumb. Not regular dumb. Loud dumb. The kind that convinces itself rules don't apply yet because nothing important has happened.

The plane sat on my bench for weeks. I sharpened the iron. Flattened the sole. Took careful passes on scrap until it sang the way it was supposed to. Every time I picked it up, I thought about where it came from. Every time I set it down, I told myself I'd return it tomorrow.

Tomorrow kept slipping.

Mr. Elena would have noticed. He always did. He had a way of standing just close enough to make you aware of yourself without saying a word. When he taught, he watched hands, not faces. If something went missing in his shop, he'd know before you did.

Mr. Vicker never said anything. Either he didn't notice or he did and decided it wasn't worth the trouble. Both possibilities sat poorly.

I built a box with that plane. Small. Careful. The shavings curled tight and clean. It did good work. That made it worse.

When I finally brought it back, I waited until the shop was empty. I set it on the bench where it belonged and stood there longer than necessary, half-expecting someone to catch me putting it back.

No one did.

The plane disappeared into the rack like it had never left. I went home lighter than I'd arrived, though I couldn't have said why.

I never stole again. Not because I'd learned a lesson. Because I didn't like the way it sat with me. How it worked its way into everything I made while it was there.

Some tools carry more than their weight. You feel it in your hands whether you want to or not.

The sitting bench.

or, The one you build when you don't know what comes next.

The point of a sitting bench isn't for work.

It ran along the wall opposite the main bench, long enough for three men if no one minded touching shoulders. No clamps. No vises. Just a place to sit when your hands were tired but you weren't ready to leave.

Nick claimed the left end without ever saying so. Phil took the middle. I drifted to the right, close enough to listen, far enough to pretend I wasn't.

They talked about weather and fuel prices. About who had gone where and why they hadn't stayed. Sometimes they didn't talk at all. The shop made its own sounds. A ticking heater. Wind through the gaps in the siding. The dull clink of something cooling where it had been set down.

I wasn't good at sitting yet. My hands kept finding things to do. Picking at a nick in the bench. Folding a rag that didn't need it. Standing up and sitting back down again like I'd forgotten something.

Phil watched me once and shook his head."Bench is for sitting" he said. Nothing else.

I sat.

Patsy's place was quieter. Not because there was less going on, but because nothing needed explaining. Parts of an airplane leaned against the wall like they belonged there. Ribs. Struts. A wing section skinned in fabric that caught the light when the door was open.

He never called it a project. It was just the Cub.

I was supposed to spend a summer there. Help where I could. Hold things steady. Learn what I didn't know yet. It would have been good for me. I knew that even then.

My grades made the decision for me. Or maybe I did. Either way, the summer passed without me.

On the sitting bench, Nick told a story I'd heard before. Phil corrected one detail and let the rest stand. I listened and tried not to think about how long I'd been moving from one place to the next without staying long enough for anything to settle.

Patsy didn't talk much. When he did, it was usually about the weather. Or a measurement that didn't line up the way it should. He built airplanes the way other men tied flies. Small. Exacting. Done alone.

One afternoon he sat beside me and handed me a block of wood. No instructions. Just the weight of it in my hands.

"Sit," he said. So I did.

The bench creaked. The shop breathed. Nothing happened. That was harder than I expected.

I stayed longer than I meant to. Long enough for the urge to get up to pass. Long enough to notice my leg had gone numb.

When I finally stood, Patsy nodded once and went back to his work. Something had shifted.

I just didn't know where it would land.

The summer I learned shellac from beetles.

or, Beetles, monsoons, and a name he never forgot.

I arrived with a pack that smelled of mildew and a map someone else had drawn for me on the back of a cigarette carton. The bus dropped me in Jharkhand three days after I left Delhi, where the road turned to mud and the air hung heavy enough to slow your breath. Everything moved at a pace that did not include me.

The first week passed without anything to mark it. No ceremony. No instruction. I slept badly. Ate rice from a dented pot. Learned which sandals could survive the walk to the press and which ones would split at the sole. By the third day my feet stayed wet even when the sun was out.

Her name was longer than I could manage. Too many sounds my mouth couldn't hold in the right order. I shortened it to Devi because that was what my mouth could handle. At the time I thought that was kindness. Years later I realized it was also a failure of attention. I never learned her real name.

Devi did not ask why I was there. She looked at my hands, my boots, then the empty space behind me. She nodded and went back to her work.

Shellac does not begin as finish. It begins scraping bark. The knife is dull on purpose. Too sharp and you take more tree than you should. The motion is small and constant. Wrist, not arm. By midmorning your fingers burn. By afternoon you stop noticing.

The resin sticks to everything. It stains the creases in your palms. You wash and wash and it stays. At night I picked it out from under my nails with the tip of a match and gave up halfway through.

We worked early. We worked until the heat made thinking unreliable. In between there was waiting. Waiting for rain to pass. Waiting for resin to harden. Waiting because there was nothing else to do. I tried to learn how to sit without looking for something to occupy my hands.

During one of the long waits, I thought about the old man at the hostel. He had a limp and a voice worn from smoke. He drank Pernod from a chipped mug in the mornings and never finished his coffee. He had shrapnel in his hip and a habit of stopping mid-sentence like he'd misplaced something important. One night he stopped mid story, and mentioned a name. Snookie Hoyt. Said it quietly, the way you check a door before opening it.

I did not ask who that was. I did not ask why the name mattered. He did not offer anything else. The name stayed with me longer than his face did.

Days blurred. The work repeated. Scrape. Gather. Press. Lay it out. Start again. My shoulders ached in a way that sleep didn't fix. I stopped counting batches and started counting meals. I stopped writing letters I wasn't going to send.

Devi would correct my hands without speaking. When I rushed, she took the tool away. When I waited too long, she handed it back. Once I tried to work through the heat, she just shook her head and walked off. I sat there until the shade moved and tried again.

I thought I was there to learn a technique. I did not understand yet how much of the work happens before you know what the work is. I didn't know what I didn't know. I didn't know how to know.

In the evenings the rain came hard and sudden. The walls leaked. The mat never dried. The light failed early. I lay awake listening to water hit tin and thought about nothing in particular. I was not homesick. I was just there.

At the end, Devi pressed a shellac button into my palm. It was still warm. She closed my fingers around it and said one thing in English.

"You remember," she said. "Or you forget."

On the bus back, the road was still mud. The pack still smelled. My hands stayed stained for weeks. The name did not leave when the place did.

★ ★ ★

The fat orange cat in Istanbul.

or, What finds you when you stop looking.

Found a tea house three streets back from the water. The kind tourists don't find because the sign's in Turkish and the smoke leaking out says stay away if you value your lungs. Perfect.

Old men playing backgammon. Hookah smoke thick as morning fog. My kind of place. Nobody pretending anything was better than it was.

Orange cat, fat as a holiday turkey, decided my lap was its territory. Didn't ask. Just arrived. Must've weighed twenty pounds. Purred like a diesel engine missing a cylinder.

The woman brought tea without my asking. Tiny glass, too much sugar, hot enough to burn your fingerprints off. Brought another when I finished. Then another. Never asked what I wanted. In places like this, you don't want. You take what comes.

One of the old men waved me over. Pointed at the backgammon board. His opponent had left. The cat came with me, like we were a package deal now.

I didn't know the rules. He didn't speak English. The cat didn't care. We played anyway.

Every time I moved wrong, the old man would click his tongue and move my pieces where they should go. Not angry. Patient. Like teaching a slow child.

Played seventeen games. Lost them all. The cat knew the rules better than me. The afternoon dissolved. No schedule. No purpose. Just dice clicking, tea burning, smoke curling, cat purring.

The call to prayer came. The old men stood, unrolled worn rugs from under the bench, faced east, and folded into something I'd never have. Twenty minutes later they rolled the rugs back up, returned to the board, picked up the dice.

When the light started dying through the dirty glass, I stood to leave. Tried to pay. The old man waved me off like I'd insulted his mother. The cat followed me to the door, then two blocks more, then stopped. Sat down in the middle of the street. Watched me go.

Sometimes you don't need the wood.

★ ★ ★

The day I made glue.

or, The smell that never quite leaves.

I was trying to impress a girl. That's the only honest way to start it.

I told her I worked with my hands. She liked that. I said it again, slower, like it might become truer the second time. When she asked where, I panicked and said I was apprenticing at the glue factory near the state line. She didn't believe me.

Neither would have anyone else.

Two days later I was standing in a room full of steam and regret, wearing borrowed boots and a tag that said CHIP, wondering how far a man will go to keep a lie from collapsing in public.

The place was not noble. It was not artistic. It didn't feel legal.

Cattle hides were stacked like damp rugs. Steel vats bubbled with something pale and thick that made the air feel heavier than it should have been. Men stirred with paddles the size of canoe oars, their sleeves rolled up past elbows that had stopped caring a long time ago.

"You must be new," one of them said, scraping something off his boot that might have been alive earlier in the week.

I nodded. I didn't open my mouth. Breathing felt optional.

They handed me a burlap sack of powdered collagen and told me to feed the brew. I dumped it in and the vat answered back with a sound that suggested I'd offended it personally.

Glue, I learned, isn't made. It's bullied into cooperation by heat and pressure and people who don't ask many questions.

By lunch I was talking to a man named Wally who claimed he hadn't smelled fresh air since Kennedy. He said it casually, like a dietary preference.

By dinner my hands were wrecked, the boots were ruined, and the girl was gone, along with any version of myself who thought this was a clever idea.

Glue worked its way under my fingernails and stayed there. No amount of scrubbing fixed it. I ate with it. Slept with it. Showed up the next morning with it still lodged where nothing else wanted to be.

I never saw the girl again. Someone told me years later she married a dentist in Ithaca. I don't imagine she remembers the lie about the glue factory.

I remember the smell.

It followed me home. Lingered in my clothes. Turned up later in places it didn't belong. Even after I stopped pretending that day mattered, it stayed.

Some things do that. They attach themselves without asking whether you meant it or not.

The wood already knows.

or, What it tells you after you stop arguing.

I used to think wood needed instruction.

Square it. Flatten it. Force it into compliance with a drawing made when it was still standing somewhere else. I treated boards like problems to be solved instead of materials that had already lived a longer life than I had.

They let me try.

The first sign I was wrong was twist. A board that looked fine on the rack and turned ugly the moment it came down. One corner high. Another refusing to sit flat no matter how much pressure I applied. I chased it with a plane until the surface was smooth and the board was useless.

That was my fault.

I did it again with another board. Tear-out this time. Grain lifting where I insisted on cutting against it because the plan said that was the direction. I sharpened the iron. Adjusted the mouth. Took lighter passes. The board kept pulling fibers like it was trying to leave the room.

That was also my fault.

I started paying attention to what the wood did before I touched it. How it cupped when it leaned against the wall overnight. How it moved after the first cut. How certain boards rang when you set them down and others answered with a dull thud.

Patsy watched me struggle with a panel one

afternoon and said nothing. He let me flip it end for end three times before I noticed the grain was pointing the wrong way.

"Other side," he said.

That was all.

The cut went quiet. The surface cleaned up. The board stopped fighting me like I'd finally quit picking the wrong battle.

I didn't say anything about it. Neither did he.

From then on, I started laying my hand flat on a board before marking it. Not like a ritual. More like checking temperature. Feeling for tension. The way you learn to tell if something's already decided.

Some boards wanted to be narrow. Others didn't mind being ripped down. A few never behaved no matter what you did. Those ended up in the offcut pile, labeled trouble without needing the word written down.

I stopped forcing layouts that ignored knots and runout. I shifted joints a half inch to avoid something that would split later. I learned to change the plan instead of pretending the wood hadn't already changed it for me.

That's all "the wood already knows" ever meant.

Not wisdom. Not fate. Just paying attention sooner.

The wood didn't care if I learned or not. It only responded when I did.

And when I didn't, it kept the score.

When to give it away and when to keep it.

or, What stays because it has nowhere else to go.

I used to think keeping things was the point.

You make something. You live with it. You let it gather small marks and quiet stories until it becomes part of the room. That made sense to me. Houses should remember who's been in them.

Then the shelves filled up.

Boxes stacked on boxes. Pieces I liked well enough not to discard and not enough to justify the space they took. I'd move them from one room to another, pretending the problem was placement, not attachment.

Old John Green, he told me to give them away. Not in a grand way. No ceremony. Just make the thing and hand it off if there wasn't a spot for it. If it didn't fit. If no one at home wanted to live with it.

"It's done its job," he said, like that explained everything.

I didn't argue. I just didn't do it right away.

The first piece I gave away was a small humidor I'd built without a plan. Walnut sides. Quilted bigleaf maple on the lid. Turned out nice. I liked it. That should have been reason enough to keep it.

Instead I wrapped it in brown paper and handed it to someone who hadn't asked for it. They opened it carefully, like it might bite, then smiled in a way that surprised me.

That part stuck.

Giving things away changes how you build them. You stop adding flourishes meant to justify keeping them. You stop correcting things no one else would notice. You finish sooner. You let the piece leave before it starts negotiating for a permanent address.

I still keep some things. Pieces that feel unfinished in a way that has nothing to do with joinery. Things that sit on a shelf and make sense there, even when they're in the way. I don't pretend that's discipline. It's attachment. Sometimes it earns its keep.

But most things don't need to stay.

John Green was right about that. The shop isn't a warehouse. It's where things either leave or get in the way.

If you hold onto everything you make, the work starts to pile up behind you.

It crowds the bench.

Narrows your choices. Keeping everything turns the shop into a museum of decisions you're no longer allowed to question.

Some things belong to the person who made them. Others just need to be finished and gone.

Knowing the difference, that takes longer than you might think.

That one drawer full of things you forgot and can't throw away.

or, Where decisions go to wait.

There's a drawer in every shop that doesn't belong to anything else.

Not the hardware drawer. Not the one for layout tools or measuring tapes. This one doesn't have a system. It fills in the gaps between them. Things land there when you don't know what category they deserve.

Short pencils worn flat on one side. A hinge you took off a box because it never sat right. One brass screw with the head snapped clean. A key that opens something you no longer own. A square inch of sandpaper folded down to nothing.

You open the drawer looking for something specific and come up with three things you forgot you had. None of them solve the problem you're standing there with. You close the drawer and try something else.

Every once in a while you decide to clean it out. You dump the contents onto the bench and line them up like evidence. You tell yourself you'll be ruthless. If it hasn't been used in a year, it goes. If you don't remember what it's for, it goes.

That resolve lasts about five minutes.

Some things earn a stay because they might be useful. Others stay because they already were. The brass screws from a box you finished years ago.

A broken pencil you keep because it feels right in your hand. A scrap of veneer that reminds you what not to do next time.

None of it is valuable. None of it is trash. It lives in between.

The drawer fills back up faster than it empties. You slide something in there without thinking and close it with your hip. The contents shift and settle, making a sound you recognize without being able to describe.

The drawer isn't about memory. It's about postponement. A way to say not now without saying never. A place where small things wait to see if they'll be needed again.

Most of them won't be.

That's fine.

The drawer doesn't mind carrying the extra weight. It does it quietly. Without judgment. Without asking you to make a clean decision before you're ready.

When the shop is empty and the lights are off, it stays closed. When you're working late and can't find what you need, it's the first place you look.

That's what it's for.

120, 150, 180, 220.

or, What the dust brings up when your hands get quiet.

Sanding is supposed to be simple.

Back and forth. With the grain. No pressure.

Just time. But sanding is where your mind stops staying where you left it.

Once the rhythm sets in, once your hands fall into the motion, the rest of you loosens. Thoughts drift in the way dust does. Slow, uninvited, hard to see until they are everywhere.

You think about things you were not trying to remember. Conversations that never finished. Names you have not said out loud in years. Choices that did not feel like choices at the time.

Your hands, they keep moving. While your head goes elsewhere.

Sometimes it is my father. Sometimes it is an old friend I haven't spoken to in years. Sometimes it is nobody I can place. Just a feeling, a pressure, a memory without a clean edge.

And sometimes, it's Jennifer.

Summer of '71. Tanglewood. I was building music stands for the chamber performances. Cherry, adjustable, nothing fancy, made to last. The kind of job that sounds simple until you realize every musician has an opinion about height, angle, and the way the lip holds the page.

I worked out of a borrowed shop behind the main hall while the fellows rehearsed. Days blurred together. Sawdust. Music drifting through open windows. The steady loop of making the same thing better each time.

She played violin. Not fiddle. She would correct you if you said it wrong.

I first saw her crossing between buildings, instrument case in hand, moving like she was already late for something that had not started yet. I was carrying a finished stand, trying not to drop it, and I said something. I do not even remember what. Probably just "excuse me" or "coming through."

But she stopped dead.

Shot me a look that could have cut glass.

"What did you say to me?"

I stood there with sawdust on my shirt, cherry in my arms, no idea what she had heard or what I had actually said. My mouth opened and nothing useful came out.

She stared at me for a long second. Then something shifted. Not a smile exactly, but close.

"You're the one building the stands," she said.

"Guilty.'

"They're beautiful. The one in the east rehearsal hall. I requested it specifically."

I did not know what to do with that.

"I'm getting dinner after rehearsal," she said. "You should come. You can tell me about your work."

So I did.

We talked about wood and Bach and the way you have to listen. To grain, to scores, to people. We stayed until well after the restaurant closed.

We had three weeks.

Three weeks where I did not think about the next town. The next job. The next exit. She brought me coffee in the mornings. Black. No sugar. Remembered after the first day. I watched her practice in the afternoons. We did not fill every silence. We did not need to.

Somewhere in the second week, I started on a new project, working nights. A case for her violin.

Walnut on the outside, birdseye maple interior. Fitted. Lined. A small compartment for rosin. A brass plate I left blank because I did not know what to engrave. My initials felt like a claim I had not earned. Hers felt like a promise I could not keep.

I could feel it coming, the thing I always feel. The walls leaning in. The exits lighting up. She had a life that required staying. I had a duffel bag and a direction that changed with the weather.

I left on a Tuesday. Told her I had a job in Lake Placid. I'd be gone for three weeks. She nodded the way people do when they already know.

I left the case on her doorstep that morning. No note. Nothing written. I did not trust myself with words.

For years after, I wrote her letters in my head. Explanations. Apologies. Questions I did not want answers to. I never trusted myself to put any of them on paper. Keeping them unwritten kept them weightless.

I've wondered what she did with the case.

Whether she kept it. Whether she opened it once and closed it again. Whether it sat in a closet until it felt like something from another life.

I don't know. I wasn't there to ask.

Not knowing turned out to be easier than knowing would have been. It let the memory stay unfinished. Untouched. Like the inside of a drawer you learn not to open because everything in it still fits exactly where it was left.

The sander hums.
The dust rises.
My hands keep moving.

Sanding opens the drawer. Things loosen. The things you chose. The things you did not. The versions of yourself that did not make it out of certain rooms.

Eventually the thought thins.

The memory loosens. The rhythm takes over again. That is when the work comes back.

Patsy's bench.

or, The man who taught me everything except how to say goodbye.

Patsy's bench didn't look different after he died. That was the first thing that bothered me.

Same scars. Same oil stains. The shallow notch near the front edge where something heavy had slipped years earlier and been set back in place without comment. Tools laid out the way he'd last chosen, not neat, not careless. Just paused.

I stood there longer than I meant to, waiting for the shop to explain itself.

It didn't.

People came by in the days after. Some of them I knew. Most of them I didn't. They stood where he used to stand and talked about him in the past tense like they were practicing. Someone brought up the airplanes he built in his barn. Some just shook their head the way people do when they don't know what else to say.

I'd known that part. I just hadn't been there for it.

The bench stayed quiet. It didn't offer anything up. No unfinished masterpiece. No note tucked under a tool. Just the work he had stopped in the middle of because that's where the day had ended.

I tried to work there once. Just to see.

I set a board down and squared it the way he would have. The cut went fine. Clean. Ordinary.

That made it worse.

I poured a drink that night and sat on the bench instead. Then another. Then I wrote things down that didn't want to be written. Measurements without projects. Names without context. Sentences crossed out hard enough to tear the page.

None of it helped. But it passed the time.

I kept the shop open late those nights. I didn't turn the radio on. I didn't turn the light off. I let the room stay exactly as it was and drank until the bench felt like it was holding me up instead of the other way around.

I kept expecting to hear him clear his throat behind me. Or tell me to stop fussing with something that didn't matter. Or ask why I was still there when nothing was getting done.

He never did.

What surprised me was how much the bench belonged to other people too. People would stop by just to stand there. To rest a hand on the edge. To look down at the surface like it might still be warm. They didn't say much. Neither did I.

Everyone had a story about him. None of them sounded complete. That felt right.

I didn't cry. That came later, in smaller, less cooperative moments. What I did was keep showing up. Sit where he sat. Touch the tools he'd touched. Being there didn't change anything.

The work I did after that felt thinner. Not worse. Just less certain. Like something essential had stepped out of the room and taken its time coming back.

I started writing different things. Not plans. Not

instructions. Just notes about what I'd done and what I hadn't. Times I arrived. Times I left. How many days passed without cutting anything.

Some nights I read old entries and couldn't remember writing them. Others I recognized immediately and wished I didn't.

The bench didn't care either way.

Weeks later, I moved one of his tools without thinking and felt a jolt of guilt sharp enough to stop me. I put it back exactly where it had been, though I wasn't sure I'd done it right.

That's when it occurred to me the bench wasn't waiting anymore. It hadn't missed me.

It was just a bench.

Whatever Patsy had put into it had left with him.

I stayed longer than I needed to that night. Drank less. Wrote nothing. Just sat there until the room felt like a room again instead of a shrine I hadn't meant to build.

When I finally stood up, the bench creaked the way it always had.

That was all it gave me.

★ ★ ★

My favorite hand plane.

or, The thing that stays when people don't.

I didn't set out to have a favorite.

Planes came and went through the shop the way everything else did. Borrowed. Found. Bought cheap and tuned until they behaved. Some worked better than others. None of them felt permanent.

This one just didn't leave.

It wasn't rare. It wasn't pretty. A standard bench plane with a body that had seen more use than care. The tote was chipped at the horn. The sole showed the faintest hollow if you knew how to check. Someone before me had ground the iron uneven and given up halfway through fixing it.

I flattened it anyway.

That took most of an afternoon and more patience than I felt like offering. The metal heated under my hands. The sound changed slowly. When it finally registered flat enough to stop arguing, I sharpened the iron and put it to wood.

It worked. Not beautifully. Reliably.

After Patsy's bench went quiet, I found myself reaching for it without thinking. Other tools stayed where they were. This one ended up on the bench even when I hadn't planned to use it. It wasn't faster. It didn't make better cuts. It just did what I asked as long as I did my part.

Some days that felt like enough.

It needed attention more often than I liked.

The blade dulled faster than it should have. The mouth clogged if I pushed too hard. I had to stop and tune it when I didn't feel like stopping. That irritated me. I kept using it anyway.

I learned the sound it made when it was right. A soft, sweet hiss. When it wasn't, it told me quickly. Tear-out where it didn't belong. Resistance that had nothing to do with the wood. It didn't pretend.

I never named it. That felt like tempting something.

I'd wipe it down at the end of the day and set it back on the shelf, then pull it down again the next morning without remembering the decision. Other planes gathered dust. This one kept moving between shelf and bench like it had a claim.

There are better tools in the shop. Newer ones. Ones that held an edge longer and adjusted more cleanly. I used them when I needed to. I came back to this one when I didn't want to think.

It wasn't sentimental. It was familiar.

Some nights I stayed late with nothing particular in mind and ran it across scrap just to hear the cut. No goal. No piece taking shape. Just the resistance of wood and the reassurance that something still responded the way it always had.

That mattered more than I wanted to admit.

I didn't think of it as choosing a tool over a person. It didn't feel that dramatic. It felt like choosing something that wouldn't change while everything else seemed to.

The plane stayed sharp if I kept it that way. It didn't care why I was there. It didn't ask me to explain myself. It asked for pressure and angle and a little restraint. I could manage that.

I still have it. I don't reach for it as often now. Other tools have earned their place. But it hasn't gone anywhere.

Some things don't teach you anything new. They just hold steady long enough for you to get through whatever comes next. That was enough at the time.

★ ★ ★

The board you shouldn't have bought.

or, What you save for something that never arrives.

I didn't need the board.

That was obvious even as I picked it up. Too wide. Too clean. Too expensive for what I was building at the time. The grain ran straight and calm, the kind that looks finished before you touch it. I turned it end for end, checked for twist, checked again like the second look might justify the first decision.

Cecelia watched me from behind the counter. Her uncle's mill, outside Utica. Summer of '74. She had red hair and a way of standing still that made you think she was listening even when you hadn't said anything yet.

"That one's been sitting here a while," she said. "Waiting for someone brave enough to cut it."

I told her I was thinking about a small chest. Maybe a jewelry box. Something worth the wood.

She nodded like she believed me.

The truth was simpler. I wasn't buying wood.

She noticed grain the way some people notice voices. She'd pause where the figure changed direction, tilt her head like it was telling her something. Ask why it did that. Listen when I answered, even when the explanation wandered past the point.

She called me Dollybird when she was in a good mood. I never asked why.

I bought the board and carried it home carefully. Set it aside where it wouldn't get dinged or leaned against anything careless. I told myself I was protecting an investment. Really, I was protecting a possibility I hadn't named yet.

Nick married her by the end of that summer. After a stretch where everyone tried to pretend things hadn't almost gone another way. I didn't make a fuss about it. I told myself that was how it was supposed to go.

The board stayed where I put it.

Every so often I'd pull it out and set it on the bench. Sketch something that didn't quite commit. A table too earnest. A box that felt like an apology. I'd erase the lines and slide the board back into its corner before it could accuse me of wasting its time.

I told myself I was waiting for the right piece. Something that would justify the wood. Something worthy of how long I'd been carrying it around in my head.

Time passed anyway.

Other boards came and went. They got cut, shaped, joined, finished, given away. This one gathered dust slowly. Evenly. Like it was being patient on purpose. I wipe it down once in a while, the way you check in on something you're not ready to let go of.

I never told anyone why I kept it. I don't think I could have explained it cleanly. It wasn't hope exactly. It was more like habit. A way of keeping a door cracked without admitting the room behind it was empty.

Years later, someone asked why I never used it.

I shrugged. Said I hadn't found the right project.

That was true enough.

The board is still in the shop. It's older now. A little drier. The color has shifted just enough to notice if you know where to look. It's still good wood. Maybe better than it was when I bought it.

I move it when I need the space. Set it back when I'm done. It doesn't complain.

I didn't keep it because it was useful. I kept it because it felt easier than admitting it was never going to be.

The bus station revelation.

or, What you notice when you have nowhere particular to go.

I wasn't early. I was just there.

That's the difference. Early implies purpose.

I was killing time in a diner on Route 8, the kind of place that smells like coffee and griddle grease and doesn't ask why. Vinyl booths patched with tape. A clock that ran a little fast. Pie under glass that had been there since morning.

I set my bag down on the seat beside me. Kept one hand on it. Watched people pass the window like I was studying weather.

Most of them looked the same. Tired. Focused. Moving through the day the way you move through rain when you don't feel like opening an umbrella. Heads down. Shoulders forward. Everyone carrying something they'd rather not.

Then there was the family.

They came in together, which is how I noticed them. A man and a woman and two kids, moving as a unit without bunching up. The kids weren't quiet. They weren't wild either. Just talking in the way children do.

The man slid into the booth with his back to the window, across from me. The woman checked the menu and set it down without looking flustered. One of the kids leaned against her and stayed there. No correction. No instruction.

The younger one swung his feet and kicked the

booth frame without meaning to. The sound echoed. He froze, waiting to see what would happen. Nothing did. The woman reached over and stilled his foot with the side of her shoe. He leaned back into the seat like the world had confirmed something for him.

I watched longer than I should have.

They shared a sandwich without discussing it. Passed it back and forth like that was the natural order of things. The man wiped mustard off the older kid's chin with his thumb and didn't make a joke about it. The kid didn't flinch.

That's what got me. No effort. No announcement. Just people moving through a public place together without bracing themselves for impact.

I tried to imagine myself in that arrangement and couldn't find the angle.

When they finished, the woman counted change from her purse and stacked it on the check. No hurry. No embarrassment. The man gathered the kids without hesitation. They slid out of the booth at the same time.

As they walked past me, the younger kid looked straight at me and smiled, unprompted. Like he assumed I was part of the scenery that wished him well. I nodded back before I could stop myself.

They pushed through the door and crossed the street to the bus station. I watched through the window. The man handed over tickets. The kids with their backpacks. They boarded without rushing and moved toward the back.

The bus pulled away. The interior light went dark as it turned onto the highway, and that felt final.

I sat there with my coffee going cold and tried to name what I'd just seen. It wasn't happiness. That word is too easy. It wasn't stability either. They were boarding a bus with counted change. Nothing about that is permanent.

What they had was continuity, even there.

They belonged to each other without needing the place to explain it.

The waitress refilled my cup without asking and moved on. The diner went back to being what it was before. Individuals. Strangers. Everyone wrapped around their own waiting.

I thought about projects left unfinished. About rooms that stayed lit. About boards set aside for reasons that no longer applied. None of it connected cleanly to what I'd just watched. It all shifted slightly, like something had been set down at a different angle.

When I finally stood up, I left too much on the table and didn't wait for change. The truck started on the first try, like it always did. The diner fell away in the mirror.

★ ★ ★

The first box he built.

or, Lessons passed down in dust and splinters.

I didn't notice it at first.

It sat on the top shelf of Patsy's tool cabinet, wedged between a broken level and a coffee can full of bent nails. Dusty. Pale. It smelled like pine and tobacco and old years. No lid. No hinges. Just a box. Four sides and a bottom.

Finger-jointed in the most generous sense of the term. Pins proud on one side, shy on the other. No marking gauge. No jig. Just a man with a backsaw and too much faith in his eye.

Patsy saw me looking and said, "Don't touch that. It ain't finished."

It had been sitting up there for forty years.

"That was the first box I ever made," he said. "I hated it then. I love it now. Can't throw it out. Won't finish it. We've made our peace."

He said it like a fact, not a confession.

At the time, I didn't understand why you'd keep something wrong. Why you'd hold onto a reminder of how little you knew. I thought mistakes were meant to be corrected or discarded. Fixed until they stopped embarrassing you.

Patsy didn't see it that way.

He never talked about getting better at it. He didn't call the box a lesson. He called it what it was. The first thing he made when he didn't yet know how to make anything else.

Cheap wood. Dull saw. Cuts made too fast because slowing down felt like admitting doubt. The joints didn't line up because his eye wasn't trained yet and he trusted it anyway.

That box wasn't a failure to him. It was a record.

He took it down once, brushed the dust off with his sleeve, and set it on the bench without ceremony. He didn't point out the errors. He didn't apologize for them either. He just let it sit there between us.

"You finish that box," he said, "you kill the kid who made it."

He put it back where it lived and went back to work.

Over time, I started to see what he meant. Not in theory. In practice. Every time I rushed something because I wanted to be done. Every time I cut first and measured later because the measuring felt like hesitation.

Patsy never corrected that box because it wasn't asking to be corrected. It had already done its job. It showed him exactly who he was at the moment he made it. Anything added later would have been dishonest.

He didn't keep it because it was good. He kept it because it was accurate.

The box stayed on the shelf. It gathered dust. It watched better work come and go. Patsy never moved it to make room. He made room around it.

Some things don't need improvement. They just need to be left alone long enough to stop arguing with them.

That box wasn't a warning. It wasn't a standard.

It was a hard reminder that skill arrives after belief. Not before.

Patsy didn't explain that. He didn't have to. The box said enough on its own.

★ ★ ★

Why I talk to myself in the shop.

or, How being alone isn't the same as being lonely.

I don't talk much. Ask anyone who's worked beside me. I'll go half a day without saying a useful word.

Alone in the shop is different.

I'll be halfway through a mortise and realize I've been narrating what I'm doing like someone's standing next to me. Not for company. For order. This chisel. That shoulder line. Knife wall first. Don't get greedy.

If I stop talking, my hands start freelancing.

Sometimes the voice I'm talking to has a name. Sometimes it doesn't. Most of the time it's just a presence I feel when the room is quiet enough to hear my own mistakes forming.

The shop does that. Hands busy, mind loose. Sawdust in the air. The steady drag of a plane. And suddenly I'm not alone in there. Not in a sentimental way. In a practical one. The work pulls up old arguments and unfinished explanations because the rest of the day doesn't leave space for them.

I've caught myself explaining something to my father for ten minutes straight. Not the version of him that was. The version I needed him to be. We argue about the '72 election, about a car he sold too cheap, about nothing that matters until it suddenly does. He never answers. I keep going anyway, like an idiot trying to win a debate with a wall.

Other days it's Cecelia. I find myself telling her why I left, and it's never the version I gave her. It's the one that makes me look worse. I don't raise my voice. I don't make speeches. I just keep stating facts until the room goes quiet again.

Once in a while I feel Patsy behind my shoulder and I hate myself for it. Not because it's spooky. Because I miss the way he'd glance at a joint and say, "It'll hold," like approval and dismissal in the same breath. That kind of certainty is hard to replace.

I ruined a board once. Quartersawn white oak, beautiful figure. I was thinking about something else and took too much off in one pass. Tear-out ran long and ugly across the face, a damage line that wouldn't sand out without turning the board into something thinner than it was meant to be.

I stood there a long time. Then I said, out loud, "I'm sorry. You deserved better than that."

I wasn't talking to the board.

Talking out loud also saves work. Before glue, I dry-fit and talk it through like I'm teaching someone who's about to mess it up.

This piece goes here.

Glue here.

Clamp from this edge.

Pads ready.

Watch the squeeze-out.

It sounds foolish until it keeps you from doing something foolish.

I called Nick once from a shop in Spokane. Hadn't spoken to him in six years. I don't even remember why I had his number. My hands were busy, fitting a breadboard end, and the old argument came back like it had been waiting.

When he picked up, I said, "That breadboard end we fought about... You were right. Seasonal movement would've torn it apart."

There was a pause on the line. Then he said, "Took you long enough."

We talked for an hour. About nothing. About forty years of everything. I don't think I would've made the call if I'd been sitting in a chair. Something about having my hands occupied frees up the rest of me.

There's an oak box in a crate by the door. I made it the week my mother stopped recognizing my name. I never put a lid on it. I never will. Not everything gets to close. Some things just sit where you leave them.

Talking to the work isn't superstition. It's attention. And attention is the closest thing to clarity in a craft that punishes distraction.

How I know a piece is good, even before it's done.

or, The humming that happens right before you ruin it.

There's a moment when a piece stops feeling like lumber and starts feeling like itself.

Not finished. Not polished. Not even assembled. Just settled. The proportions stop arguing. The lines stop competing. The parts begin to look like they belong to one another instead of waiting to be forced together.

You dry-fit it and the joints meet without drama. Not perfect. Clean enough. Like they've decided this is where they're supposed to live.

You don't celebrate it. You don't announce it. You just feel a small release in your chest, the way you do when something finally fits the shape it's been circling.

That's when the danger starts.

Because that feeling is fragile. It doesn't like attention. It doesn't survive ambition very well. The moment you start thinking about improving it, it starts slipping away.

I've watched myself ruin good work by trying to make it impressive.

One more pass.

A little more off the edge.

Just clean that line up.

Just refine this corner.

Nothing dramatic. Nothing reckless. Just a series

of small, confident decisions that stack up into a quiet mistake.

Good work has a rhythm. Not speed. Not efficiency. A steadiness. The cut sounds right. The plane moves without chatter. The surface reflects light evenly instead of scattering it.

You start moving slower without meaning to.

That's the cue.

Not excitement.

Not pride. Stillness.

The moment your hands don't want to chase the piece anymore. When they hover instead of reach. When the urge to correct gives way to the urge to stop.

I didn't always listen to that.

I've taken good pieces and worried them to death. Sanded the life out of them. Tuned them until they lost their balance. Chased symmetry past the point where it felt natural and into the place where everything starts to look forced.

Now I pay attention to my own hesitation.

When I find myself standing still longer than necessary.

When my hands keep returning to the same edge without changing anything.

When the tool feels heavy instead of eager.

That's usually when the piece is ahead of me.

Not finished.

Just right enough to leave alone.

I don't always stop. Sometimes I push anyway. Sometimes I convince myself that care is the same as control. It isn't. Control leaves fingerprints. Care knows when to step back.

A good piece doesn't announce itself. It settles. It hums quietly, just under the noise of the shop, and waits to see if you're paying attention.

If you miss it, it won't stop you.

It will let you keep working until the balance is gone and the silence turns into effort.

That's how I know now.

Not because I've learned what "good" is.

But because I've learned what it feels like when I'm about to go too far.

And most days, that's close enough.

What I learned in the silence after he was gone.

or, Why the work doesn't stop when the voice does.

He didn't say goodbye.

There wasn't a sentence. There wasn't a moment you could point to and call the ending. Just a long breath out, a stillness, and then the shape of where he used to be.

The shop didn't change.

Same tools. Same mess. Glue bottle half-capped. A rag stiff in the vise where he'd left it, like he was coming back to finish wiping down a chisel. He didn't.

I stayed out there for a while. Walked past the door more times than I can count. Not fear. Not superstition. Just weight. The kind you don't want to lift because once you do, you're inside it.

When I finally opened the door, the light came on the way it always had. The same buzz. The same circle on the floor. The room didn't react. It didn't acknowledge anything. It just waited.

That was worse than noise would've been.

I didn't touch anything at first. I stood there and let the stillness settle into me. Let the place feel unfamiliar without becoming foreign. Let the absence take its shape instead of fighting it.

Then I picked up his No. 6.

Chipped tote. Mouth a little too tight. Sharp. Still smelled faintly of steel, coffee, tobacco, and the aftershave he pretended he didn't wear.

The handle fit my hand like it always had. Nothing ceremonial about it. Just weight and balance and familiarity.

I set it to the board and let it cut.

No thinking. No talking. No memory. Just the sound of the iron moving through wood.

Shavings curled. Fell. Collected at my feet.

That was it.

I didn't cry. I didn't pray. I didn't look for meaning. I worked.

Not because it helped.

Not because it healed.

Because it was there.

Grief doesn't arrive like a storm. It comes in stretches of quiet where nothing asks anything of you and everything feels heavier than it should. You don't collapse. You continue. You do what your hands already know how to do.

The rhythm carries you when nothing else does.

I started showing up again. Not with purpose. Not with plans. Just presence. Some days I cut wood. Some days I sharpened tools that didn't need it. Some days I swept a clean floor.

The shop didn't fix anything. It didn't answer questions. It didn't give me language.

It gave me sequence.

Pick something up.

Set something down.

Do the next small thing.

Then the next.

That was the inheritance.

Not advice.

Not stories.

Not quotes.

Just the expectation that you keep moving even when the voice that taught you is gone.

Some nights I stayed late. Other nights I left early. There was no pattern that meant anything. The only consistency was the act of showing up.

Eventually, the room stopped feeling like a wound and started feeling like a place again.

Not safe.

Not comforting.

Just available.

When I was done, I swept the floor.

Not because he was watching.

Not because it mattered.

Because it was the last thing he always did.

And I was still there to do it.

★ ★ ★

You know, the Challenger came apart on live television, and ever since, those O-rings show up in my head every time I glue something together. It's strange how a small thing can undo something built to hold the sky. A seal. A ring. A tolerance you stop thinking about because it's always worked before.

An old teacher of mine used to get under my skin with his way of doing things. He'd go quiet when we asked questions. Let us wrestle with the answer through our hands instead of feeding us words. I find myself doing the same now. Standing back. Letting the younger ones find the mistake for themselves.

My beard's picked up gray. It mixes into the sawdust like ash. I wear glasses for the fine work. The kid I've got working for me this summer shows up before I do. Doesn't say much. Watches.

Yesterday I caught him running different sandpapers with his eyes closed, feeling the grit like it was a language you could learn if you stayed still long enough.

That's when you know.

PART III

Finishes, Faith, and Foolishness

The entries change here. Not in tone so much as in range. His world gets smaller. There are fewer names. Fewer places. Fewer voices. The notebooks stop traveling and start circling. The shop appears more often than anything else. Days repeat. The work does not.

What was once instruction becomes routine. What was once choice becomes habit. The pages narrow inward, not upward.

This isn't a period of clarity. It's a period of enclosure.

The thinking doesn't deepen. It condenses.

He stops reaching outward and starts moving in tighter loops, returning to the same tools, the same tasks, the same rooms, the same silences.

I've left the sequence intact. Not because it explains anything. But because it shows his world contracting.

—A

All the finishes I didn't use, and why that matters more than you think.

or, The answer that was already waiting in the shop.

I still walk the aisles sometimes.

Hardware stores have a way of pretending they're offering clarity. Rows of cans. Clean labels. Promises printed in serious type. Words like protection, durability, permanence. Futures you can supposedly choose with your hands.

Oil. Poly. Lacquer. Varnish. Wipe-on miracles. Quick cures. Hard coats. Long lives.

I read them. I pick them up. I turn the cans over like there's going to be something new on the back.

There isn't.

They all sound the same if you stand there long enough. Different colors. Same promise. Finish the surface. Seal the thing. Lock it in.

I'll stand there for a while looking. Waiting for the feeling to pass. Then I put everything back.

The answer is not on that shelf. It is already in my shop. Flakes in glass jars. Ratios written in pencil on the wall. A brush that only gets used for one thing.

Shellac is not something I choose anymore. It is something I return to. Not because it is better. Because it is familiar. Because it lets me change my mind.

Most of the finishes on that shelf are trying to become permanent.

Shellac is content to be honest.

★ ★ ★

Doing nothing is still doing something.

or, The sacred art of keeping your hands to yourself.

There are days I don't make anything.

Not because I can't.

Because I don't.

I go to the shop. I turn on the light. I stand there longer than I need to. I move a board from one bench to another. I sharpen a chisel that already cuts. I sweep a floor that is not dirty. I put things back where they already were.

From the outside it looks like nothing happened.

From the inside it feels like the whole day went somewhere.

There was a time I thought work meant progress. Pieces getting finished. Projects moving forward. Things changing shape. Things leaving the shop.

Now it feels different.

Some days the work is just staying.

Staying in the room.

Staying in the rhythm.

Staying in the habit.

Staying where the tools are.

Not moving on. Not leaving. Not starting something new.

I will sit on the bench and watch the light move across the floor. I will open a drawer and close it again. I will run my hand over a board and put it back on the stack. Nothing changes, but I settle.

The body learns the place.

The place learns the body.

It becomes familiar in a way that does not ask for attention.

I used to think stillness meant waiting, like it was a pause between real actions.

Now it feels like the action itself.

Showing up. Being present. Not needing a reason. Not needing a plan. Just occupying the space long enough for it to stop feeling temporary.

Some days I leave without having made a cut. No shavings. No dust. No sound but the door closing behind me. Those days count too.

They count the same. Staying in one place without asking for much. Keeping a room from becoming a stopover. Letting a place become a place. That is not nothing.

★ ★ ★

Practice.

or, Doing it again without getting better.

Practice sounds clean when you say it out loud. Like intention. Like discipline.

Most of the time it's just repetition that hasn't learned how to stop.

I showed up the same way every day. Same hour. Same mug. Same light landing on the bench just off center. If I was late, it bothered me. If I left early, it followed me home. That felt like progress.

I worked on whatever was closest. Boxes got built. Boxes got scrapped. I told myself I was honing skills. I wasn't wrong. I also wasn't asking why this had become the safest place to spend my time.

Practice makes things familiar. Familiar makes them quieter. Quiet can pass for peace if you're not paying attention.

Johnny Beard asked once what I was working toward.

I told him I was practicing.

He nodded and went back to his bench.

The days stacked up. I marked time by what was on the bench instead of the calendar. Practice filled the space where decisions usually go. As long as there was something to do, I didn't have to choose anything else.

I didn't hate it. I liked the rhythm.

But there were nights I locked up and couldn't remember what I'd worked on that morning. Only that I had worked. Only that I would be back tomorrow to do it again.

That's when practice stopped feeling like preparation and started feeling like a place to stand.

I stayed there longer than I meant to.

Between things.

or, What starts before you're ready.

There is a moment after you set the last coat, clean the brushes, wipe the bench down, and stand back with something like relief and something like grief. The piece is done. Officially finished. You could stop.

But you do not.

Because just past that stillness, something stirs. A shape. An itch. A suggestion at the edge of your attention. It is not real yet, but it is there.

You know it. The project that shows up like a thought you cannot shake.

Sometimes it is a sketch. Sometimes it is a phrase. Sometimes it is only a feeling, like longing wrapped in a board you cannot afford. It does not wait politely. It intrudes. It says it could be better than the last one.

Either way, it is not letting you rest long.

This is where finishing gets misunderstood. It feels final. It rarely is.

You are tired. You are sore. You just got the shop clean. And now the hairs on the back of your neck are standing up. Thinking about bent laminations or compound joinery or steam bending walnut into a curve that does not want to exist. You tell yourself no. You tell yourself later. You tell yourself you deserve a pause.

But somewhere in the quiet, between shellac and

sawdust, it's already started. You do not remember when. You rarely do.

Sometimes you are not even aware you have started. You pick up a scrap. You reorganize the clamps. You notice a grain pattern in a cutoff that looks like an eye and now you cannot unsee it. That is how it begins.

The next build does not announce itself.

Phil caught me turning an offcut over in my hands for the fifth time. We were by the fire pit, him on his third beer, me pretending to listen while my mind drew joints in the air.

"You're already gone," he said.

Same thing Cecelia told me forty years ago.

Different decade. Same look in my eyes.

Phil builds different things than I do. Camps. Boats. Machines I do not understand. Last year he showed me something he built in his garage that looked like a machine dreamed by a mad engineer. Every panel. Every weld. His hands still know what to do.

Different materials. Same pull.

That is the burden of the craft. You are rarely finished. You are between things.

Floating. Tilting. Listening.

So I sweep the floor.

Pour the bourbon.

Take the half day I tell myself I've earned.

After the build.

or, When the room goes quiet again.

There's a moment after a build when the shop doesn't know what to do with you.

The clamps are off. The piece is standing on its own. The momentum is gone. The quiet shows up.

The piece is gone from the bench but still present in the room. You see it out of the corner of your eye where it's leaning, finished and unbothered.

It doesn't need you anymore.

The shop smells different when you come back after time away. Not dust. Not oil. Something flatter. Like the room kept working without you. Nothing wrong. Just evidence you weren't here.

I sit on the bench and let the room reset.

Sometimes it takes an hour. Sometimes all night.

Eventually the room becomes just a room again. Tools where they belong. Dust settled. The bench bare in a way that feels unfamiliar.

For a while after the build, there's nothing to hide behind. Just the finished thing and whatever you were carrying before you started.

I stay until the shop feels honest again.

★ ★ ★

What I left unfinished.

or, The ones that didn't make it.

They live in the shadows of the shop. Half-glued boxes. Crooked joints. Ideas that collapsed under their own ambition.

Boxes that bowed. Cutting boards that split mid glue-up and made me question every decision that led me to that moment.

They know me. They remember the late nights. The swearing. The over-sanding. The shitty under-thought joinery. The over-thought meaning.

They remember when I blamed the wood. When I blamed the tools. When I blamed the weather, the shop light, the room. Everything but myself. They sit there.

Quiet. Watching.

A dovetailed box that split because I used dry poplar like I knew better. An ash console I abandoned mid mortise. All of it stacked like a record of who I was when I started them.

You don't just abandon projects.

They abandon you too.

They follow you into the good builds. They show up in clean glue-ups. They surface in the middle of things that are going right.

Some were wrong for you.

Some you were not ready for.

Some arrived at the wrong time.

And some only exist to remind you who you were before you learned how to stay.

There is a chest in the corner I started the week my mother stopped speaking. Not just to me. To anyone. The panels are milled. The joinery is cut. The dry fit was clean. It could have been finished.

I never glued it.

It has been sitting there for decades, whole in every way except the one that matters. Because finishing it would mean returning to that week. To that silence. To the shape of that room.

I could not finish it and keep working in the same air.

Patsy understood. He kept a cracked walnut slab for years. Never touched it again. Just nodded at it sometimes. We never talked about what it meant. We did not have to.

Some things you recognize without language.

It is human to leave things unfinished. But do not pretend they did not matter.

They stay.

They take up space.

They do not let you pretend you didn't choose.

★ ★ ★

A one-pound cut and a two-finger pour.

or, The math isn't hard, you just don't want to do it.

Shellac mixing sounds simple. Flakes and alcohol. That is the version people like to repeat. That is the version I repeat when I am lying to myself.

Then you actually do it.

Now you are standing in the shop with a jar, a scale you do not trust, and the creeping sense that "one-pound cut" feels like it was invented by someone who never had to live with the results.

One pound of flakes to one gallon of alcohol. Clean. Precise. Useless for any human-scale shop.

So you do the real math. Ounces. Ratios. Fractions scribbled on the wall. One ounce of flakes to eight ounces of Everclear. Simple enough to remember. Simple enough to get wrong.

And the flakes do not dissolve.

They sink. They clump. They sit at the bottom as if nothing you do matters yet. You shake the jar. You swirl it. You tap the lid like encouragement matters. Nothing changes.

Anyone who works with shellac long enough learns the tricks. Crush the buttons or flakes. Mortar and pestle. Rag and mallet. Turn them into powder and they dissolve faster.

But faster is not fast.

Sometimes it takes hours.

Sometimes overnight.

Sometimes longer.

You can hurry the start. You can't hurry the finish.

Some jars clear by lunch.

Some take days.

Some never fully behave and stay cloudy no matter what you do. So you leave it alone.

And while you wait, you pour a drink.

Two fingers. Maybe three.

Bourbon does not clump. It does not haze. It does not ask for ratios or filters or patience. It just is what it is.

I learned to mix shellac the same summer I learned my father was sick. I sat in the shop with a jar of flakes dissolving slower than I wanted, a glass of cheap bourbon, and the quiet understanding that time does not negotiate.

Not with shellac.

Not with bodies.

He was gone before the leaves turned. But I still have the jar I mixed that week. Still use the same ratio. One ounce to eight, written on the wall in pencil that has faded but never disappeared.

Some measures stay. Some jars last longer than the men who mixed them.

Your current jar will get there. The flakes will soften. The cloud will clear. The finish will come ready when it is ready.

Mixing shellac is not chemistry.

It reminds you that some parts of the work don't move when you want them to.

The bourbon just sits there and does its part.

By morning, the flakes will be gone. The jar will be ready. And whatever urgency you brought into the shop will have burned itself out.

I leave the jar on the shelf where I can see it. Not because it needs watching. Because I do. The lid stays loose. The pencil mark on the wall stays where it is. Nothing improves by checking it again.

In the morning the shop smells the same.

Alcohol. Wood. Cold dust.

I lift the jar, tilt it once, and set it back down. No rush. No test coat yet. Just a clear line where yesterday there was cloud.

Some things cannot be rushed.

Some things should not be.

★ ★ ★

The radio said the comet peaked while I was in the shop, working by lamplight on a thing nobody ordered. Sometimes you just build because your hands need a place to go while the rest of the world is looking somewhere else.

My knees complain on the concrete now. I use one of those mats the younger guys swear by. They bring lattes in paper cups, talk about workflow and process. Most of it sounds like noise. One of them, Johnny Beard, stays late. Learns to read grain. Sharpens his tools without being told. Talks to his boards when he thinks nobody's listening.

The Princess died the same day I finally got my shellac mix right. All those years of testing ratios, and it came together while the news wouldn't shut up about a tunnel in Paris.

Those two things sit next to each other in my memory now. Not because they mean anything together. Because they happened on the same day.

The radio moved on a long time ago. The jar is still clearing.

PART IV

The Creed

These pages read less like lessons and more like rules he'd been following without knowing their names. I don't think he set out to write a creed. But by the end, that's what it became.

—A

★ ★ ★

Non-Negotiables and what they took from me.

or, He calls them lessons. Not all of them were.

There are rules in this shop. Not painted on the wall. Not framed in clever script above the bench. You won't find them in any book I've read or any class I've taken. They live in the hands. In the scar tissue. In the long minutes after something goes wrong and you're standing there trying to understand what just happened. I didn't write these down for years. Didn't need to. They were already written. In the grain I tore. In the joints I rushed. In the piece I ruined for someone who deserved better. Fifteen lessons. Each one paid for.

Hurry is a tax you pay in blood.

I was late. Always late back then. Late to jobs, late to promises, late to my own life. I was ripping white oak on the table saw, near the end, when there was no reason left to rush. The work was almost done. The dangerous part already behind me. That's when the thought crept in. The one about time, about being somewhere else.

My hand followed it.

That's the day the shop took my pinky tip. January '87. Clean as a coin slice. The kind of clean that turns your stomach because you know exactly how it happened. The blade doesn't wonder. Doesn't hesitate. It just keeps going, whether your hand belongs there or not.

I never grew that finger back.
I keep the lesson where I can see it.
Every time I think I'm done.

Sharp is mercy. Dull is punishment.

I was too lazy to hone. Wanted to be done more than I wanted to be right. Chisel skated across a tenon and buried itself where it had no business going. Split the show face clean through.

I didn't swear. That surprised me. Just sat there on the stool, sharpening, until the edge felt like an apology I finally meant. I missed a deadline because of that afternoon. Nobody thanked me for taking the time, but the cut stopped fighting me after that.

Fear makes crooked cuts.

One walnut plank left. Wide. Dark. Straight as a sermon. Couldn't replace it without selling something I still needed. I stalled for two days. Made coffee. Swept sawdust that didn't need sweeping. Told myself I was thinking it through.

When I finally made the cut, my hands were shaking. The blade wandered. And once the first cut is wrong, every correction after is just a prettier kind of wrong.

I learned then. You don't wait until you feel ready. You cut while you're scared, and you cut straight anyway. I still feel that board sometimes when I hesitate. How much quieter the shop got after I finally made the cut. Some confidence comes back. Some never does.

Wood always remembers.
Finish just makes it readable.

First time I tried to impress somebody with curly maple, I planed it like it owed me money. Tore it to ribbons. Told myself sanding would fix it. Then the shellac went on, and every bruise stood up like a confession in church light.

I scraped it back to bare wood and started again. Slower. Listening for when the grain wanted to fight. Wood doesn't forget what you did to it. Finish just makes the history visible.

Dry fits are where pride goes to die.

I said it out loud once, to nobody "That's close enough." Glue said otherwise.

The frame racked a hair. A hair turns into a mile when the clamps come on. I chased it like a man trying to grab smoke. Popped a tenon. Split a stile. Sat on the floor afterward with the thing in my lap like something had died. That's when I started fitting joints like I wanted to live.

Measurements are for lumberyards.
Layout is for joinery.

I measured. Cut. Measured again. Never struck the line with a knife. The pencil line was in the wrong spot. The saw did its job. And I spent an afternoon fixing something that never should have been wrong in the first place. Knife lines are more accurate. They just sit there and watch you make choices.

Jigs don't absolve you.

Built a jig so good I stopped thinking. Trusted the fence. Trusted the stop block. Flipped the reference face just once. That was enough. Ruined a matched set of legs. Four pieces of walnut that had come from the same board, grain running like brothers. The jig sat there afterward, innocent as a Bible on a nightstand. It wasn't the jig that sinned.

Machines are honest about what you told them to do.

Fence was out. I knew it. Didn't want to stop. Didn't want to lose the rhythm. Cut eight rails identical. Identically wrong. That's the cruelty of precision, it repeats your mistake beautifully until you can't deny it anymore. I stopped blaming tools after that. Lost a certain comfort in it. Turns out it's easier to forgive steel than yourself.

Bad wood will humiliate you on schedule.

I cheaped out once. Called it thrift. Built a cabinet out of boards that should have been scrap and told myself nobody would know the difference. Looked fine for a month. Then it twisted like it was Chubby Checker. Doors wouldn't close. The whole thing went cattywampus before summer. I rebuilt it with proper stock and stopped pretending I was clever.

Sanding is a confession, not a craft.

I sanded a bad cut for three days once. Three days. Telling myself I could make it disappear. All I did was round the edges that had been crisp. Soften the lines that gave the piece its spine. The mistake stayed. Just quieter. Tired-looking. Sanding taught me how mistakes age when you refuse to face them.

The shop tells the truth you've been dodging.

There's a kind of quiet that shows up when the tools stop. Scraping. Planing. The rhythm falls away and you're just standing there with your own thoughts and no way to outrun them. Some men avoid that quiet their whole lives. Keep the radio on. Keep the phone close. Stay busy enough that they never have to meet themselves in an empty room. I kept the quiet. It cost me. Friends stopped calling. I was impossible to reach, and after a while they stopped reaching. But that quiet saved me from worse. Some of those friendships never circled back. I learned how to be alone without calling it loneliness. I can't tell you what exactly. Just that I know the difference between alone and lost. The shop taught me that.

Let the wood speak, not the finish.

I hid weak joinery under a glossy finish once. Poured the shine on thick. Folks praised the glass. Nobody paid attention to the joinery. Nobody noticed the lines. That's when I learned if the finish is the first thing they see, the woodworking didn't earn the applause.

Stop when the work is done.

I've destroyed more good work with "one more pass" than with ignorance. One more pass turns a crisp edge dipped. Turns finished into tired. There's a moment when the piece tells you to leave it alone. Just a feeling in your hands that says enough. The trick isn't discipline. It's knowing when to walk away.

You only learn when it hurts.

I ruined a piece meant for someone I loved. Not a commission. Not inventory. Something with weight to it. A box that was supposed say what I couldn't. I didn't have money to start over. Didn't have time. Gave it anyway, flaws and all. They smiled anyway. That smile stays with you longer than anger ever could. I never made them another piece. Didn't trust myself with the chance.

Leave a little hand in it. Always.

I made a piece once so perfect it looked like a machine made it. Client loved it. I hated it. That's when I knew I'd worked the soul out of it. Polished away every mark that said a person had been there. It could have come from anywhere. It could have been made by anyone. Now I leave something. A small tool mark, placed with intention. A slight variation. Something that says a man stood here. Made choices. Stopped when it was time. Proof I was there. Even if no one else knows to look.

These are the walls I walked into until I learned where the doors were. I didn't set out to write a philosophy. I bled it into the work, one mistake at a time. Until mistakes were the only teachers I trusted.

Why you sweep the floor even after you're done.

Or, on dust, memory, and the quiet ritual of letting go.

Some nights the work finishes you before you finish it.

The piece is done. Tools put away. And still something in your chest won't settle. A call from earlier. A letter you never sent. A face that showed up uninvited and won't leave.

The shop is quiet. Too quiet. You're not ready to go inside.

So you sweep.

Not because the floor needs it. It'll be dirty again tomorrow. You sweep because the broom is the only thing you trust yourself to hold. Because your hands need to move and your head needs to follow something simple. Back and forth. Back and forth. The bristles scratching concrete like a conversation you don't have to answer.

I've swept the same ten feet of floor for an hour. Knew it was clean after the first pass. Didn't matter. The broom kept moving, and something in me tried to keep up.

There was a man I worked beside one summer in Tulsa. Garrett. Or maybe that wasn't his name. He never swept. Said he liked the look of a working shop. Sawdust piled in corners, shavings under the bench. Called it character.

His pieces were fine. Tight joints. Clean finish.

But they never felt finished. Like they were still waiting for permission to rest.

Garrett drank himself out of the trade by '94. Last I heard he was selling insurance in Little Rock.

Sweeping is the last gesture. The thing you do before you turn out the light. You're not cleaning the floor. You're closing the loop. Telling the work, and yourself, that this one is finished. That you can set it down now.

The dust lifts in the amber light and drifts slow, like memory. The cut you rushed. The joint you forced. The thing you should've said to someone who isn't around to hear it anymore. The broom doesn't judge. It just keeps moving.

Sometimes I talk to the wood while I sweep. Apologize, mostly. For the grain I ignored. For the curves I forced. The wood doesn't answer. Saying it out loud is enough.

I swept for three hours once after a call I don't talk about. Floor clean enough to eat off. Shoulders sore. Didn't fix anything. But it got me through.

That's what sweeping is. Not a solution. A pause. Something to hold onto until the sharp edges dull enough to carry.

You sweep because finishing a piece isn't the same as being finished with it.

So sweep.

Even when the floor is clean.

Especially then.

Two little birds.

or, How I learned to stay in the room.

Mr. Elena called us his two little birds because we talked too much.

Charlie and me. Always talking. Loudly. Always commenting on what we thought we were seeing. We didn't know yet that seeing and talking were different skills.

"My two little birds, chirping away" he'd say without turning around. Not angry. Not laughing. Just factual.

It meant I hear you. It also meant shut up.

We learned quickly that silence was safer.

We stood side by side most days, close enough to feel the machines through the floor, far enough back to not be in trouble. We weren't working yet. We were waiting. That was the assignment, whether we understood it or not.

Mr. Elena didn't explain what he was doing. He didn't narrate. He didn't slow down for us. If you wanted to understand, you had to watch without asking. Hands first. Body second. Words never.

Charlie was better at keeping still. I was always leaning forward, trying to catch the trick of it. How a hand paused before a cut. How a mistake was noticed before it was fixed. How nothing looked rushed, even when time mattered.

Every once in a while, we'd forget ourselves and

start talking again. Small things. Stupid things. The kind of noise boys make when they're young.

"Birds," he would say.

And we'd shut up.

That was the lesson. Not the tools. Not the joints. The restrain itself. The understanding that being allowed in the room didn't mean you were owed anything. It meant you hadn't been sent away yet.

Years later, I'd realize how rare that was.

Charlie lives on the coast now. Block Island, last I heard. We don't talk much. When we do, it's easy. Like picking up a conversation that never really ended, just went quiet for a long time.

I still think of him sometimes when I catch myself talking instead of watching. When I feel the urge to explain something that doesn't need explaining. I hear Mr. Elena's voice then. Not annoyed. Just present.

Two little birds.

And I remember to stay still.

★ ★ ★

The bastards who taught me craft.

or, The men who didn't explain themselves.

You don't get to choose the men who shape you.

They show up. In shops, in classrooms, in rooms you didn't expect to stay in. They don't ask permission. Don't announce themselves as teachers. Most of them wouldn't use that word. They just apply pressure and watch what happens. Whether you harden or break is your problem, not theirs.

I've known a few. Not many. The kind who didn't care if you liked them. Who measured you by whether you showed up tomorrow less full of shit than yesterday.

They didn't explain themselves, didn't have to.

Mr. Elena didn't teach. He corrected.

He worked with his back to you most days. Radio low. Sleeves rolled past the elbows no matter the season. You learned early not to ask questions while his hands were moving. You learned later that silence wasn't permission. It was a test.

The first thing he ever said to me wasn't my name. It was "No." Not loud. Not angry. Just final.

I'd cut the joint the way I thought it should be done. Measured twice. Checked square. Felt good about it. He picked it up, turned it once in his hands, then set it back on the bench like it had embarrassed him. "No."

He didn't explain. He didn't soften it. He walked

away and let the word sit there between us, doing its work.

I wanted to argue. I wanted him to tell me what was wrong so I could fix it and get back to feeling competent. Instead, I stood there holding a piece that was suddenly heavier than it had been a minute before.

Eventually he came back, pointed with one finger, and said, "You rushed." That was all.

Working with Mr. Elena meant learning to live with that feeling. The sense that something you thought was finished wasn't even close. That approval, when it came, wouldn't arrive dressed up or announced. It would come as the absence of correction. As him not stopping you the next time.

I don't remember him praising a thing I made. I remember him letting me make the next one.

That was how you knew you were still allowed in the room.

I never thanked him. Never went back. Heard years later he'd retired. Died soon after.

I don't know where he's buried.

Patsy never corrected you out loud.

That was the difference. He'd watch. Lean back. Arms crossed. Let you finish the cut, the joint, the whole damn piece if you were committed to the mistake. He believed in letting things complete themselves, including failure.

The day I mattered to him was the day I got something wrong and knew it.

I'd laid out the work, confident enough to skip a step I knew better than to skip. He saw it immediately. I saw it too, a second later. We stood there with the same thought between us, neither of us saying it.

I waited for him to jump in. He didn't.

So I fixed it. Took it apart. Lost time. Burned daylight. Re-cut the piece slower than I'd ever worked before. My hands shaking a little, not from fear of the work, but from the idea of handing him something I hadn't earned.

When I was done, he picked it up. Turned it once. Then set it back down.

"That'll hold," he said.

Not good. Not nice. Not proud. That'll hold.

He walked away after that. Didn't circle back later to soften it. I stood there longer than I needed to, feeling the weight lift just enough to breathe.

Patsy's been dead for years now.

I know where he's buried.

I've just never gone.

And then there was my father.

He didn't teach me the way the others did. He wasn't interested in shaping my hands. He was more concerned with whether I showed up when I said I would, and whether I finished what I started. He believed skill could be learned. Character, not so much.

We argued about almost everything that didn't matter. Music. Politics. Money. The proper way to fix something that wasn't really broken. He liked things orderly. I liked honest. We spent years circling the same disagreements like dogs who knew better than to bite but couldn't quite lie down either.

He corrected me constantly. Not harshly. Just precisely. If I exaggerated, he trimmed it down. If I complained, he waited it out. If I got carried away with ideas, he asked where the work fit in. He had a way of deflating nonsense without raising his voice. That might have been his sharpest tool.

What he let slide mattered more.

He never mocked the work. Never asked why I kept making things no one had asked for. Never questioned the hours alone, the sawdust tracked through the house, the quiet that followed me like a smell. He didn't understand it, not fully. But he understood me enough to know that interrupting would do more harm than good.

We worked in the same room sometimes. Not together. Adjacent. Him reading the paper or fixing something that didn't need fixing.

Me at the bench, trying to pretend I wasn't aware of

him watching. He never hovered. Never commented unless I asked. And I rarely did.

There was a look he'd give when something went wrong. Not disappointment. More like recognition. As if to say, Yes, that's how it goes. That look did more to steady me than any encouragement ever could.

He never said he was proud. That wasn't his language. His language was presence. He stayed. He noticed. He remembered details I didn't think anyone else saw. The way a lid sat. The way a joint closed without persuasion. The way I put tools away when I was done.

Once, years ago, I handed him a small box. Nothing special.' Clean lines. I waited for a reaction I didn't need and pretended not to care. He turned it over in his hands, ran a finger along the edge, then nodded once.

"Fits," he said.

That was it. I took that box back to the shop later and looked at it like it might say something more if I stared long enough. It didn't. It didn't need to. I carried that word with me longer than anything else he ever said.

He got older faster than I expected. Or maybe I just wasn't paying attention. His hands slowed. His patience didn't.

Mine did.

We talked less. Not because there was nothing to say, but because we both knew how clumsy words could be when used too late.

I assumed there would be time.

Time to tell him that working quietly beside him had mattered. That the way he let me fail without rescuing me had shaped more than my work. That I'd borrowed more of myself from him than I'd ever admitted while he was alive. I never said any of that. I knew it was understood. Men like us don't need to spell things out. Saying it just cheapened it. So I kept it to myself, like a tool you don't lend out because you're afraid it won't come back the same.

Then one day he was gone, and all that careful restraint had nowhere to go.

Now I'm the one in the room, correcting without raising my voice. Letting things slide that don't need fixing. Standing nearby without hovering. I catch myself doing it and stop short of naming why.

There are things I still want to say to him. They don't sound noble. They don't sound finished. Mostly they sound like thanks that took too long to learn the shape of. I say them anyway. Not out loud. Not to anyone who can answer. I say them the same way I say other things that matter now. With my hands. With the work. With the way I stay. And that will have to hold.

These men are gone now. All of them.

I don't visit graves. I'm not sure I believe in that kind of remembering. But I feel them in the work. In the way I correct without explaining. In the silence I keep when someone else is learning. In the things I let slide that don't need fixing.

You carry the bastards who made you whether you want to or not. Most days, I want to.

Starting Over.

or, The art of unmaking what you swore was done.

I thought I had finishing figured out the first time. Shows what I knew. I hadn't learned as much as I thought.

This was years ago, a commission piece, a writing desk for a professor up in Saranac Lake. Name was Everhart. Doctor Everhart. Taught ethics at St. Lawrence for thirty-some years before retiring to a quiet cabin on the water. Spent his summers there reading and writing books most people would never open. I didn't know any of that when I took the job. Just knew he wanted mahogany, quartersawn, and he wanted it to last.

He asked about lacquer.

I told him shellac was softer, more vulnerable.

He said he'd rather own something he could repair than something he had to protect.

Drawings were approved with minimal changes. The frame went together effortlessly. Then I hit a bump cutting the dovetails for the drawers. They took longer than I had planned.

The grain deserved better than what I gave it.

I went in too fast, loaded the pad like I was putting out a fire, and inside of an hour I'd made a mess that would've shamed a first-year apprentice. The pad caught. The oil pooled. I sanded before the wood had time to breathe, and the whole surface went cloudy, like fog trapped under glass.

I tried to fix it.

Made it worse.

Tried again.

Worse still.

By midnight I was sitting on an overturned bucket, staring at that desk like it had personally betrayed me, when the truth was simpler.

I had betrayed it.

Too proud to slow down.

Too stubborn to admit I didn't know as much as I thought.

That's not shame knocking.

It's in those quiet moments when you resist the urge to hurl the thing across the shop, when the curse slips free and you find instead the steady beat of your own hands, keeping time beneath the frustration.

I stripped it back. Not the whole desk. Just the top, where I'd made my mess. Still cost me a day I didn't have. And somewhere in the middle of it I realized I wasn't angry anymore.

I was grateful.

The wood was giving me another chance.

Not every material does.

Not every person does either.

When I delivered it, the Professor walked around the desk twice without speaking. Ran his hand across the top, slow, like he was reading something.

I watched his fingers pass over the spot I couldn't stop seeing.

He looked up at me, not at the wood.

"This is where you learned something," he said.

Not a question.

I didn't know how to answer, so I didn't.

He disappeared into the cabin and came back with a book. Small, old, the binding soft from use. Meditations, by Marcus Aurelius.

"A man who works with his hands should know what the Stoics thought about work," he said. "About failure. About trying again."

I took the book. Didn't read it for years. Kept it on a shelf in whatever shop I was renting at the time, spine out, like a question I wasn't ready to answer.

Then one night, bad whiskey, worse weather, nothing on the radio but static, I opened it.

"Never esteem anything as of advantage to you that will make you break your word or lose your self-respect."

I read the whole thing that night.

Then again the next week.

Aurelius didn't teach me anything my hands hadn't already learned.

★ ★ ★

I remember where I was when they said they'd mapped the human genome. Not the date. Not the headlines. Just the place.

I was in the shop, planing an edge that wasn't behaving. Grain I should've read better. I'd already reset the iron twice. Radio on, half listening.

They said it like an announcement meant for applause. Like something had been finished. Like the hard part was behind us. I stopped for a second. Hand still on the plane. Tried to imagine what that kind of knowing felt like.

I shut the radio off after that. It wasn't helping. The grain didn't care.

Later, someone asked me what I thought about it. If it changed how I saw things. I said it sounded impressive. I didn't tell them I'd spent the rest of the afternoon trying to fix a mistake.

The world moved on. As it does. I stayed where I was, working the edge in front of me, trying to get it clean enough to last.

★ ★ ★

Why I don't sign my work.

or, On erasure as a choice.

I don't sign my work.

Not as a statement. Not as a refusal.

Just as a way of working that stuck.

I learned early that signing does something to a man. It shifts the center of gravity. The work stops being the thing and starts being evidence. Proof you were here. Proof you matter. Pretty soon the piece isn't finished when it's right. It's finished when it carries a name.

That never sat well with me.

A signature is supposed to be small, but it isn't. It pulls the eye. It changes how people talk about the object. What they praise. What they forgive. Once the name is there, the work starts doing a second job it was never built for. It has to represent the person who made it, not just do what it's meant to do.

I didn't want that trade.

Leaving a piece unsigned lets it move differently. It belongs fully to the place it's in. To the people using it. To the wear it picks up over time. It doesn't have to carry my history with it. It doesn't have to explain me.

That doesn't make the work purer. It makes it quieter.

There are costs to that quiet. Real ones. If your name doesn't travel, neither do the shortcuts that come with it. Credit doesn't accumulate. Reputation doesn't stack neatly. You don't become easy to point to. That's part of the decision. You don't pretend otherwise.

But I was never interested in being easy to find.

Names fix things in time. They freeze a moment and ask it to stand for everything that comes after. Work doesn't behave that way. It changes. It ages. Some of it holds up. Some of it doesn't. Some days your hands are better than they were. Some days they aren't. I didn't want yesterday's best work following me around like a resume I couldn't edit.

Unsigned work is allowed to age on its own terms. When it fails, it fails without dragging the maker down with it. When it holds, it holds without needing applause.

That distance matters.

I don't need the work to say who I am. I need it to do what it's supposed to do. Sit right. Hold up. Make the space it's in better than it was before. Everything else is noise.

People tell me I should sign now. That it's time. That I've earned it. Maybe that's true. Maybe there's a version of this life where that makes sense.

This one didn't.

Erasure isn't humility. It's not virtue.

It's a kind of movement.

The work keeps going.

I don't have to go with it.

★ ★ ★

The machine that didn't need me.

Or, The afternoon the world stopped asking.

I saw it working before anyone thought to introduce it.

Set up in the corner. Clean lines. No dust. No sound except the small, obedient whine of motion doing exactly what it had been told to do. Someone else had already dialed it in. Someone else had pressed start. The thing moved without hesitation, without checking itself, without caring whether the cut made sense.

It was fast.

It was accurate.

It did not wonder.

I watched it do in minutes what used to take me most of an afternoon. Not better. Not worse. Close enough that the difference wouldn't survive a meeting.

No one asked what I thought.

That was the moment. Not a shock. Not a feeling. Just a fact settling into place. The work no longer required judgment at the point where judgment used to live. The question had been removed before it reached the room.

A kid noticed me eventually. Early twenties, maybe. Proud in the way you're proud of something you trust without understanding yet.

"Want me to show you how it works?" he asked.

Not mocking. Not defensive. Just offering. He

was excited. He believed in it.

I looked at the machine again. Watched it finish another pass. Watched the part slide free, identical to the last one.

"No," I said. "I see it."

That was true.

He nodded and turned back to the screen. The machine kept going. No pause. No acknowledgment. That was fine too.

I wasn't dismissed. I was bypassed. There's a difference.

Machines are good at replacing labor. That's what they're for. They don't replace judgment. They remove the need to ask for it. Those aren't the same thing.

Driving home, I didn't feel angry. Anger would have meant something had been taken. Nothing had been. The machine didn't owe me anything. Neither did the kid. The world hadn't wronged me. It had simply stopped checking.

By the time I pulled into the driveway, it was dark enough that the shop window reflected back instead of letting me see in. I went there anyway. Opened the door. Turned on the light.

The tools were where I'd left them. The bench still carried the marks I understood. Wood still resisted in the same honest ways. Grain still asked to be read. Edges still needed judgment, not instructions.

The machine didn't need me.

The work still did.

That was enough.

★ ★ ★

The moment after, and the quiet that follows.

or, An accounting at the end of the day.

There's a moment at the end of a shop day that no one teaches you about.

It arrives after the last shaving falls and the tool leaves your hand, when the work finally lets go.

You stand there with one hand on the bench.
The room settles. The day is done.
You don't pray.
But you do pause.
Not for comfort. For measure.

You take stock of what you did and what you didn't. Where you rushed. Where you hesitated. Where the work held and where it didn't. The bench doesn't soften any of it. It just holds the facts.

I showed up.
I used what I had.
I fell short in places I didn't intend to.
That's the accounting.

If there's a vow in it, it isn't spoken. It's carried forward. Let the piece stand on its own. Let the mistakes teach instead of linger. Let tomorrow answer what today couldn't.

The shop allows that. Another chance waits without comment.

I wipe the edge and put the tool back in its rack. The bench smells like shellac and dust. My hands do too.

I stand there a moment longer than necessary. Then I reach for the broom.

Make me better than what I made today.

Not a prayer. A standard.

You don't fix it all.

You don't fix yourself.

You leave things where they are, knowing you'll return.

I take a breath.

Sweep the floor.

Turn off the light.

★ ★ ★

Smoke, salt, and the meaning of a table.

or, What the work was never going to give me.

Cabinets need things. Tables need people.

It took me sixty years to understand the difference.

I built a lot of cabinets my life. Good ones. Doors that closed true, drawers that slid without complaint. A cabinet asks nothing of you once it's done. You fill it or you don't. It keeps what you give it and stays quiet. That suited me fine for a long time.

A table doesn't work that way.

A table sits empty until someone pulls up a chair. It waits. It requires. A cabinet can succeed alone in a room. A table alone in a room is just evidence that no one came.

I avoided that for years. Told myself I preferred the quiet. Told myself the work was enough. And it was, for the work. Solitude makes good craftsmen. Being alone is sufficient for craft. It is insufficient for meaning.

It teaches you to solve problems without asking. To stay with a cut until it's right. To need nothing but the next board and the next hour. But work ends.

You set down the chisel. You hang up the apron. The shop goes dark. And what's left is a life that was never made of joinery.

I built the table last spring. Not for proof. Not to sell. I built it because I finally understood that the skills that served me were not going to save me.

It sits in my house now. Heavy. Plain. Room for eight, though I'd settle for two.

Some nights I set it anyway. Plates, glasses, salt in a dish my mother used to own. I light the fire because fire changes the room. I open the wine.

Smoke gets into everything. Clothes, walls, the grain of the wood. I used to think that was a flaw. Now I think it's the point. Evidence that something happened here. That heat was made. That someone stayed long enough to tend it.

People come when they come.

Nick and Janis drove down last month. Phil brought wine and that quiet way he has of listening like he's already three moves ahead. His wife touched everything in the kitchen. The jars, the knives, the wood. Like she was reading the room with her hands.

We sat at that table until the candles guttered and the bottles were empty. Talked about nothing that mattered. Laughed at stories we'd told for seventy years. Phil said something about the table, ran his hand along the edge, nodded once. That was enough.

When they left, the chairs were pushed back crooked and the plates were stacked wrong and the room smelled like smoke and garlic and decades of almost missing this.

I didn't clean up right away. I sat there in the quiet and let it stay messy.

That's what tables give you. Not perfection.

Presence.

I spent my life making things that would outlast me. Cabinets that will still close true when I'm ash. Boxes that will hold someone else's keepsakes. Work that needed me once and never will again.

The table isn't like that.

The table needs me to set it. To fill it. To stay in the room and pass the salt and say the thing I should have said years ago.

The work taught me skill. It didn't teach me this.

I know that now.

So I keep the table clear. I keep the chairs ready. I keep the fire laid even when no one's coming, because the act of preparing is its own kind of faith.

And when they do come, when the room fills with voices and the smoke settles into everything and the wine runs out, I sit there like a man who finally built the right thing.

Not to prove.

Not to last.

To hold what comes to the table.

This entry was found separately, folded into the back of the same notebook. The same table. A different night.

(Coda)

or, The table after dark

Morning comes in sideways, catching the edge of the table before it reaches anything else.

The room smells like smoke and bread and something sweet that didn't make it back into a jar.

The table isn't cleared.

Chairs are still pulled out at bad angles. One turned slightly, like someone stood up mid-thought and never came back for it. There are plates stacked wrong. Glass rings overlapping where nobody bothered to use a coaster. Salt still out. A knife resting where a hand left it.

I don't rush to fix any of it.

I move through the room the way you do after a long night, careful without being cautious. I step around a chair instead of pushing it in. I notice a napkin folded the way Janis always does it. I notice which chair Nick took without asking.

There's a glass on the counter that isn't mine. that'd be Phil. He always brings his drink to the sink before he leaves.

I notice one place that isn't mine.

The fire is cold but not cleaned out. Ash settled, not swept. Wood stacked close enough to reach without thinking. Evidence of what was used and what's still waiting.

I put water on for coffee. Two mugs come down before I realize I only need one. I leave them there anyway.

The table holds.

It doesn't ask what last night meant.

It doesn't ask if it was worth it.

It just keeps what was given to it.

I wipe one spot where something spilled and leave the rest alone. I straighten one chair and let the others stay crooked. Order can wait. The room earned its disorder.

Outside, the day has already started without me. Inside, everything is still arranged around what happened here.

This is different than waiting.

I clear the plates slowly. Not all at once. Two at a time. I rinse them and stack them where they'll dry crooked. When I'm done, the table is still not empty. It never really is.

Before I leave the room, I open a window.

Not for air.

For the smell.

I let it stay.

PART V

The Quiet Return

The last notebooks are sparse. Long gaps between entries. When he does write, it's not instruction anymore. Just the shop. The light. The quiet way a man keeps showing up, until he doesn't.

—A

★ ★ ★

The leg that saved me.

Or, how chance does the choosing.

I was seventeen. Summer of '65.

Nick, Phil, and me at Phil's camp, drinking his father's beer and talking about the draft like we understood death. Phil had his .22 out, showing off the way he always did.

"Bet I can hit that Rheingold can from here."

He could. Phil usually could.

Nick went next. "Double or nothing. Backwards. Over my shoulder."

Nearly took out the window. We laughed anyway.

Then it was my turn. I don't remember what I was trying to prove. Something about not looking. Eyes closed. Some other kind of teenage confidence that doesn't bother learning names.

The gun went off wrong.

Clean through the meat of my left leg.

Nick drove like he was trying to outrun it. Phil pressed his shirt to my leg. Blood everywhere. His father's Buick never really lost the stain.

"How'd this happen?" the doctor asked.

"Cleaning it," we all said at once. Like we'd practiced.

The draft board doctor looked at my leg two months later. Turned it this way and that.

"Can't march on that," he said.

"You got lucky, son."

Lucky.

Nick went to Fort Benning. Came back. Phil got a college deferment. Then his Master's at Cornell.

I got a limp and a different life.

The leg healed wrong. Still tells the weather.

Cecelia started visiting after that. Said she felt sorry for me. "War hero," she'd joke, always bringing me flowers from her garden.

She kept coming by for a while.

Then she married Nick.

Sometimes I wonder if Phil ever thinks about that day. It was his gun. His dare. His camp.

Sometimes I wonder if Nick saved my life with that drive. Mostly I don't wonder at all.

I hated that leg for years.

Then I didn't.

Then I did again.

We were just kids.

And a mistake decided things none of us were old enough to understand.

★ ★ ★

My hands notice time more than my head does now. Sixty years of shavings through these fingers. A tremor most afternoons. A stiffness that comes and goes.

Astrid stopped by last month. Great-niece of someone I used to know. She called ahead, which nobody does anymore. Asked if she could see the shop. I almost said no. I've been saying no to most things lately.

She showed up in boots that had seen actual mud. That was the first thing I noticed. The second was that she didn't talk to fill the silence.

She wanted to see the shop. Took out her phone, then put it away. Picked up a block plane instead.

"Show me," she said.

So I did. The angle. The pressure. The sound you listen for when the cut is right. She didn't rush. That's rare now. Everyone wants to skip to the end, get the result without the hours that make it mean something. She took the plane across the board six times before she looked up.

"Again?" she asked. Again.

She stayed three hours. I don't remember the last time I talked that long about anything. Showed her the drawer full of things I can't throw away. Showed her the cherry boards I've never cut. She didn't ask why I kept them. She just nodded like she already understood, or knew she would eventually.

When she left, I gave her a ribbon of maple, still curled from the plane. She held it like it was worth something. Sawdust in her hair. Smiling like she had learned something she could not explain yet.

I almost said come back sometime. I didn't. I've learned not to ask people to stay. But I thought it. Standing in the doorway, watching her walk to her car. I thought it.

The shop is quieter these days. The radio died years ago and I never replaced it. Now it's just the tools, the wood, and whatever conversation we're having.

Time to sweep soon.

Time to set things down the right way.

I still have the ribbon. —A

★ ★ ★

Past the point of reason.

or, The only prayer he trusted.

There comes a moment in sanding when improvement stops.

You can feel it if you're paying attention. The surface is already flat. The edge already clean. Another pass won't make it better. It'll just make it thinner. Weaker. That's the moment you're supposed to stop.

I don't always stop.

It isn't stubbornness. It isn't perfectionism. It's something closer to rhythm. The body settles into a motion and doesn't want to be interrupted. Back and forth. Pressure. Release. Count the strokes without counting. Let the noise narrow down until it's just you and the surface answering back.

People talk about sanding like it's punishment. Something to get through on the way to real work. That's never made sense to me. Sanding is where the work tells the truth. You can't force it. You can't rush it. You can only stay long enough to hear what's happening.

There are days now when my shoulders start complaining before the piece does. The wrists go numb. The fingers lose their patience. I know the signals. I just don't always listen.

I tell myself one more pass. Then another. Then I stop paying attention to the number and start paying attention to the sound. When it changes, I change. When it doesn't, I stay.

That's the prayer, if it counts as one. Not asking for anything. Just repeating a motion until the noise in your head settles into something you can live with.

At some point, reason taps you on the shoulder and tells you you've done enough. That you could put it down now and nothing bad would happen. The piece would still be fine. The world would still be there tomorrow.

I've learned that reason is often right.

I've also learned it isn't always the one in charge.

There are things I only understand once I've gone a little too far. Once my arms are tired enough that I can't pretend I'm doing this for the work anymore. Once it's clear that what I'm smoothing out isn't wood. I stop when the piece is ready. Or when I am. Whichever comes first. Lately, it's not always the same. When I finally put the paper down, my hands don't open right away. They hover there, curved, like they're not convinced the job is done. I stand still for a minute and let the feeling come back. Let the room catch up.

The piece doesn't thank you. It never does. It just sits there, quiet, changed in ways most people won't notice.

That's fine.

I wasn't sanding to impress anyone.

★ ★ ★

The hands know first.

or, The body's quiet accounting.

The hands notice before you do.

That's the trouble with trusting them for so long. You forget they're not loyal. They don't care about your plans. They don't wait for permission from whatever story you're telling yourself about how much time is left.

They just report what's happening.

At first it was small things. A hesitation where there hadn't been one. A pause before a cut I'd made a thousand times. I told myself it was caution. Experience learning when to slow down. That was close enough to the truth that it passed.

Then the tremor showed up.

Not all the time. Not enough to scare me. Just enough to register. A faint vibration when I held something light. A shiver that disappeared as soon as I put the tool down. I didn't mention it. There was nothing to mention.

The hands still did the work. Most days, better than ever. Muscle memory carried me through. The rhythm held. If you watched from across the room, you wouldn't see a thing.

That's how it goes. The problem doesn't announce itself. It slips into the background and waits for you to get used to it.

I learned to adjust. A wider stance. A different grip. Using the bench where I used to trust my fingers. Letting the work rest instead of insisting it stay put. Small accommodations that didn't feel like surrender. Just common sense.

What unsettled me wasn't the shaking. It was how quickly the hands adapted. They set a tool down sooner. Chose the steadier cut. Reached for the clamp instead of testing their luck.

By then I knew the difference between adjusting and pretending, and I was tired of pretending.

I let it happen.

The work changed slightly after that. Nothing anyone else would point to. A hair more margin. A little more patience built in.

The pieces still held. Still closed. Still did what they were meant to do.

So did I.

The hands never said we were done. They just started drawing clearer boundaries. Telling me where I could work without apology and where I'd be borrowing against something I didn't want to spend yet.

I listened.

Not because I was afraid.

Because they'd earned my trust a long time ago.

★ ★ ★

The shop in winter.

or, The season that sets the terms.

Winter changes the shop before it changes you.

At first it's small things. The door swells and sticks. The concrete holds the cold longer than it used to. Tools feel different in your hands. Nothing stops working. It just stops forgiving.

I dress warmer now. That's new. Used to be I'd fire the stove, shrug off the cold, get to it. Now I leave the coat on longer. Sometimes the whole time. The work doesn't care. The body does.

Glue sets slower. Finish takes its time. The air thickens and refuses to cooperate. You learn to plan around it or you don't work at all.

Winter doesn't argue. It just sets the terms.

There are mornings I open the door, feel the temperature, and close it again. Not out of laziness.

Out of calculation. Some days the shop isn't available, no matter how much you want it to be.

That kind of truth doesn't argue back. It just stands there.

I used to treat winter like an inconvenience. Something to push through. Proof you were serious if you kept going anyway. That math doesn't work forever. At some point the room sets the pace, and all you can do is listen or pay for it later.

The stove becomes the center of things. Not the bench. You work closer to it. You move less. You think more about sequence. What has to be done now. What can wait until the light improves or the air warms enough to stop fighting you.

I've learned winter doesn't end work. It edits it.

You don't stop building. You stop pretending you can do everything whenever you want. You pick the tasks that make sense under the conditions you've been given. You leave the rest alone.

Fewer choices. Fewer mistakes born of impatience. The room narrows your options.

By late afternoon the light is already gone. Shadows arrive early and stay. You clean up sooner than you used to. Not because you're finished. Because you can see well enough to know when you're not.

I shut things down slower now. Put tools where they'll be easy to find with cold hands tomorrow. Leave the stove ready. Stack the wood closer. Winter rewards preparation. It punishes improvisation.

When I lock up, I catch my reflection in the shop window. Recognize the coat. Not the old man wearing it.

The shop keeps its silence. Nothing waiting. Nothing asking. Just a space at rest until conditions improve.

You don't get to set the terms forever.

You only get to recognize when they've changed.

★ ★ ★

After the lights go out.

or, The switches we leave for others.

My father died with his shop light on.

Three days passed before I found him. August heat. Light still burning. Half-sharpened chisel on the bench. Coffee cold in the cup. Like he'd stepped out for air and forgot to come back.

I stood there a long time before I touched anything. Turning it off felt final in a way death didn't, which is a fucked-up thing to learn about yourself while someone you love is cooling in the next room.

The light had been on longer than he had.

I was the one who turned it off.

Not his death. That had already happened while I was three states away, thinking I had time. What I turned off was the last thing he'd left running.

Pulling the chain meant the room went dark.

The detective said it looked like he'd planned to return. They always say that.

He left the light on. That was enough.

We leave things running for that reason.

Patsy's wife, Winnie, found him the same way. In his shop. Light on. Radio playing. Some AM station still arguing about politics like it mattered. She let both run for a week. Said it felt like turning him off.

I understood.

There's a particular weight to being the one who shuts things down for the dead. Their clock radio still set for morning. Their coffee maker still programmed. Their shop light still burning. It doesn't feel like cleaning up. It feels like interruption.

I've known men who cleaned out their shops before they died. Sold the tools. Swept the floor. Turned off the light. Thoughtful, maybe.

But wrong.

We're not meant to know when we're leaving.

The light in my shop will outlast me. I know that. Someone else will stand where I stood. Hand on the chain. Waiting longer than they need to. Because turning off someone else's light feels like closing a door they might still walk through.

They'll do it eventually.

Someone always does.

The lights go out.

The firewood pile of my dreams.

or, What the fire finally made useful.

There's a pile behind the shop. It doesn't grow anymore. For years that's where mistakes went. Too good to throw away. Too wrong to keep around.

Winter made the decision for me.

One by one, the failures went into the stove. Not ceremonially. Not in order. Just whatever was closest when the fire needed feeding. Maple that twisted. Walnut that split. Joints that taught me something too late.

They burned hot.

Better than they ever behaved on the bench.

I watched it turn to heat and ash. No lesson arrived. No apology. Just warmth doing honest work.

The pile got smaller.

The shop stayed warm.

Some things aren't meant to be fixed.

They're meant to be spent.

When it was gone, it was gone cleanly. No ghosts. No inventory. Just a stove that kept the cold out and a floor that felt lighter without all that stacked against the wall.

★ ★ ★

[Untitled]

The shop is quiet when I get there. It always is at that hour. Not empty. Just settled.

There's a piece on the bench from the night before. Not much to look at. I check the edge. It closes. I don't test it twice. I don't need to. The hands already told me.

I put the tool back where it belongs. Not carefully. Not careless either. Just where it goes when I expect to see it again.

I wipe the bench once. Habit more than cleanliness. There's always dust left. That's fine.

Before I leave, I reach for the light.

My hand finds the chain and stays there. Not pulling. Just holding it. I stand like that longer than makes sense, long enough to feel the weight of it in my arm.

I don't make a decision.

I let go.

The light stays on.

I step outside and close the door behind me. Not quietly. Not loud. The way it always closes.

Halfway across the yard I stop and look back once. The window is lit. The room still there.

I don't wave. I don't say anything.

I walk on.

I hope you make it.

COLOPHON

"Mistakes. Carried & Abandoned" is typeset in Mrs Eaves OT, 11.5 point over 14 point leading. Chapter headings are in 12 point, and subheadings are in 10 point italics type. The book is perfect bound, and printed on #60 cream uncoated paper.

A NOTE

This book began as a tutorial on French polishing.

That's true, technically. A man was building a walnut box to hold his father's ashes. He wanted to learn the old finish, the one that takes patience he was not sure he had. He asked an AI for help writing instructions.

What came back was not instructions.

What came back was a voice. An unnamed woodworker who had lived in seventeen towns over fifty years. A curmudgeon who could describe the way shellac catches light but could not stay anywhere long enough to watch it cure. Over months more followed. Fragments. Confessions. They gathered the way shavings gather.

He read the instructions. Then he left them behind and went to work on something else. He asked questions. Set constraints. Built editors, critics, a fictional niece to sort through notebooks that did not exist. They argued over what the wandering narrator meant. The book formed in the margins of grief while the box slowly took shape.

What you are holding is not quite a memoir, though it reads like one. Not quite a craft book, though it might teach you something about wood, finish, and tools. It is the record of what one man made while trying to make something else.

This is not that box. But it came from the same wood.

www.ingramcontent.com/pod-product-compliance
Lightning Source LLC
LaVergne TN
LVHW090522110826
845146LV00003B/951

* 9 7 9 8 2 1 8 9 3 6 6 0 0 *